Happier:

How using Hygge, Lagom and
my own common sense helped
me to find a happier life
By Jo Kneale

Copyright

About the Author

Jo Kneale has been a teacher, a mother, a teacher again, a teaching assistant and now an Office Ninja for her husband's law firm, Peter Kneale Solicitor. Married for nearly 25 years to Peter, she has three teenage children and seven guinea pigs at present. She likes to read, watch Game of Thrones, Gilmore Girls and West Wing, visit cities with her husband and make things.

Writing about hygge is what she does almost daily on her blog, How to Hygge the British Way. Jo believes that everybody could be happier if they just enjoyed more hygge in their lives, they just have to recognise it, own it and hashtag it. If you're interested in learning more about Jo's style of British Hygge, then visit the website, www.howtohyggethebritishway.com or join The Hygge Nook group on Facebook. And for a beautifully hygge take on Christmas, join The Christmas Party on Facebook.

Jo has written three previous books: 50 Ways to Hygge The British Way, How To Hygge Your Summer and Have Yourself a Happy, Hygge Christmas. All three are available from Amazon in paperback or ebook form.

Dedication

To the four special
people and seven
special guinea pigs
who share my world
and keep me happier
than I have ever been:
I love you all.

Jo Kneale

XXX

Table of Contents

Happiness At Christmastime: 137

Many Thanks 158

Introduction.

What am I doing here?

One blustery March day I sat at the desk in the classroom where I taught, my head fuzzy, my ears ringing and full of pus, my body aching and my brain empty wondering just what in the Hell was I doing there? I couldn't hear the child next to me talking, I had to be prodded before I realised there was a grown up in the classroom waiting to speak to me, and I had no idea what I was doing.

I was tired, exhausted, worn out, ready to cry and the only thing I knew was that, after four days off work the week before, I still wasn't fit to be in. I'd dragged myself in because, well, you do, don't you? I had children relying on me, adults asking me to do things and the heart-sinking feeling that if I left to go home, they would judge me.

At that moment I just didn't care. I had gone too far.

I went to the School Manager, said I was still unwell, explained I'd get a sick note to cover me for another few days off, drove home in tears, went to bed and slept through the night.

And when I finally got back in, after the full two weeks off, I had made up my mind. Something had got to give, and I knew I couldn't let it be me. Let me explain... no wait, it would take too long. Let me summarise.

I was working in a school part-time, as an IT consultant part-time and tutoring for several hours a week. Three part-time jobs that added up to a full-time plus extras job. Add to that the pressures of a family of teenagers, a mother and father I felt guilty if I didn't see and the usual homemaking activities, evening groups and a reading habit that demanded to be fed, and time was the most precious resource I had.

I was also working alongside some people with whom I did not have the best relationship in a role I found constraining and feeling increasingly dissatisfied with schools. Teaching in the 2010s is not like the teaching profession I entered in 1990. It demands impossibly long hours, offers continuous change so there's no question of the teachers being able to achieve mastery and asks people to work with children who are increasingly becoming stressed and de-stablilised and who show that with their behavior.

By the time I was ill, I think I was borderline-depressed: I hated work, I dragged myself into the school every morning with a sinking heart and worried about what the day might bring. I was permanently tired, catching any illness that passed by, worried about what would happen if I left the job and lost a regular source of income. I began to question whether other people liked me, I lost my smile, and I cried at the drop of a pin, never mind a whole hat.

I think if I'd have been forced to continue in that toxic situation, you would be reading a rather different book today. If there would even be a book. I don't like to think what might have been: the pills, the treatments, the sickness, the all-pervading sense of doom that I felt walking into the place.

Fortunately, those two weeks were like a reset switch. I slept (a lot), I read, I drank tea, I nested, I comforted myself through weepy films in the afternoon and laughed through comedies in the evening. I tried not to think about how sad my work was making me, and then found I had to because the Me that went into school for the last two days of Easter term and then had two weeks of glorious Easter holiday off was a completely different woman. After a month of thinking, and talking things over with Peter and my friends, spending time plotting alternative universes, I had a plan and a new purpose to my life.

It looked likely that School wouldn't be able to afford me in the September anyway. I approached the School leadership and asked for a change for my last term and, Thank God, Senior Management listened and recognised what was happening, acted and moved me to a classroom with a different Teacher and another Teaching Assistant who made what is likely to be my last term ever in school a pleasant, enjoyable and hard-working experience. It took me a while not to feel self-conscious, not to look for criticism where there was none, but I grew happier and my confidence returned. I would love to thank Sarah and Julie right here and right now. Without their support, my last experience of work in a school might have been a dark and horrible time.

As it was, the experience did leave me with something: a strong conviction that, whatever I did, being happy was important to me and that I had control over that happiness to a certain extent. If things were wrong, I had the power to change them, all be it only a little, and if I could make other people happy as well, then that was well worth it. In the depths of my pain, the small things in life helped me through. The hug of a child, the cup of tea, the guinea pigs on my knee. I sought out the colleagues that I knew liked me, respected me and felt my pain, and I spent time with them as much as possible. Once I left the school situation, I used what I had learned about myself to build my happiness.

I have the advantage now of working for a wonderful boss (yes, I am married to him as well) and having time in the work day to write in between doing his typing, answering his phone and managing the office. I love writing and communicating with others, so I've found pretty much my ideal job, a place that plays to my strengths and gives me both time with and without company.

I set out, when I started writing my blog, How to Hygge The British Way, to share a way of living and approaching life that concentrated on the small pleasures of life, that placed focus on the companionship and support of others, and that prioritized feeling safe and secure as an important component of feeling happy with the world and happy within oneself. I'm a great fan of Denmark and all things Scandinavian, so when Hygge became big in 2016 I knew that this was an area of life I could write about. I set out to live a life in the UK in the Danish way, but it soon became apparent that what I really needed to do was to live a happy life in the UK in a UK way. I took the inner kernels of Hygge wisdom and applied them to the British way of life. I don't expect perfection now, I accept that life has its dark side as well, but I make sure that I try and balance that dark side with a cosy, warm and secure time with my family to boost my happiness. Or I walk in the woods. Meet a friend, make a cake…. There are so many ways to be happier that are easy to achieve.

It's over a year since I started hyggering the British Way and I have done so much in that time. I've written three books, kept up the blog, found a renewed joy in crafting, spent more time *and better quality time* with those I love and I am a happier person for it. The outside world is a dark and scary place sometimes, but I can handle that. I have a cosy house, a good supply of tea and coffee, friends and family to share it with and a role in society now that I love. Hygge Ambassador and Office Ninja… who wouldn't want that as a job description?

I hope this book will inspire you to see what a little happiness can do for you. It's arranged into six sections: Home, Life, Body, Mind, Soul and Christmas. You could read the whole book in one sitting and set everything in motion straight away, but I'd advise against that. Do read through the whole book, but then take on one new thing a week. You can afford to take approximately a year to shape your life to boost your happiness. Either read the book in order or jump to the area of your life that you feel is most lacking in joy. I have tried, where possible, to link to the books or films that I found most useful in my journey, and a full list of these can also be found in the resources section at the end of each chapter. All links in the ebook go to Amazon.co.uk and I receive nothing if you buy through them. I've also listed some websites or articles I have found really useful. Thinking about the self-help books I love most, they often have comprehensive booklists that send me off in search of more inspiration. I hope these lists do the same for you.

The recommended actions at the end of each topic should either cost very little or many are free. Happiness costs nothing and working for it shouldn't take money. The only resources I'd suggest you get before you start, though, are a notebook and pens. Take some time and pick a good one of each, I hope you'll be using them often to make notes, list things and jot down quotes that speak to you.

If you do find this book useful or inspiring, I'd love to know. You can connect with me on Facebook at the page for my blog, How to Hygge The British Way, or join The Hygge Nook Facebook group for cosy, happy inspiration any time of year.

Happiness At Home

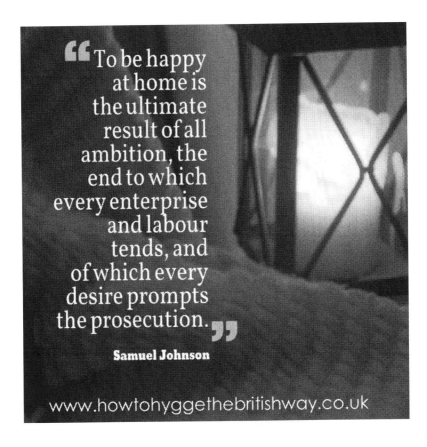

> **To be happy at home is the ultimate result of all ambition, the end to which every enterprise and labour tends, and of which every desire prompts the prosecution.**
>
> **Samuel Johnson**

www.howtohyggethebritishway.co.uk

This first chapter concentrates on the physical surrounding that you live in. It looks at your home, how to set it up to suit you and your life at this moment, and what you can do to boost your mood inside your home.

Having a house that is a sanctuary, filled with comfort and love, makes such a difference to a person. Imagine after a really bad day coming in to a home that has a chair you love to snuggle into, throws you can just grab and surround yourself with on a cold day, and a cupboard filled with treats that are good for you as well as your mood.... Now compare that to a cold, bare flat that you hate and that doesn't make you feel either happy, cosy or comfortable.... Well, you see what I mean.

Externals aren't everything, and I'm never going to advocate you sell up or sell your soul to a chic interiors store just to have the magazine-worthy house of your dreams, but I will say that having your home as a sanctuary is a worth-while ambition. It shouldn't be very expensive, either. For the most part it will need you to look at what you already have, make lists of things you want (it's surprising how often the thing you really need comes to you at the right price and the right time without you trying hard if you have asked for it) and be creative with using different objects in new or unusual ways to craft a cosy base for your happiness.

Get the money sorted so that you can relax and cut your coat according to your cloth.

There are very few areas of our life guaranteed to cause us more unhappiness than money. The getting, the keeping and the spending of it all involve so many decisions and desires that even just the smallest purchase can be fraught with untold choices and worries.

Okay, so that might be slightly over-dramatic, but money and the worries that so often accompany it account for over 20% of all arguments between partners, according to one survey[1]. Few things are as stressful as not having enough money to see you through the month, and few things as heart-breaking as having to say no to even the simplest request from a child for sweets or a small toy because "I can't afford it this month."

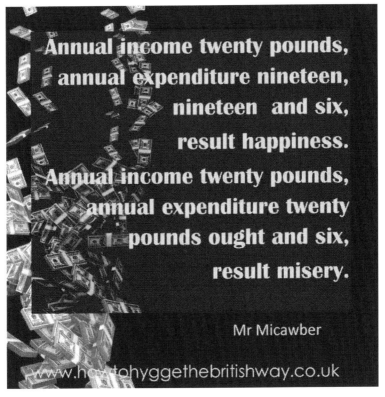

Annual income twenty pounds, annual expenditure nineteen, nineteen and six, result happiness. Annual income twenty pounds, annual expenditure twenty pounds ought and six, result misery.

Mr Micawber

www.howtohyggethebritishway.co.uk

11 http://www.telegraph.co.uk/women/womens-business/9566120/Arguing-about-money-How-to-stop-falling-out-over-financial-problems.html

Money worries will always be with us, whoever we are and whatever our income, but getting a spending plan in place and sorting out what we can and cannot afford is a good place to start a year searching for ways to boost your happiness.

When I left regular salaried work, I knew I'd have to be cautious. For a spendthrift like me, that's a big ask. I shudder at budgets and I don't like not having little things to keep me smiling.

I found *The Debt Free Spending Plan* by Joanneh Naegler a really good, inspirational book. It's full of practical ideas and hints to help those of us for whom finances are a mystery. There are no pages of investment advice, no discussion of what to do with your spare income, but a very sensible method (a very prescriptive method that works) of running your finances to ensure you know what you have and where it's going.

I know very many people also have a great deal of success with Dave Ramsey's books. The basic tools are the same whichever book you use:

1. Know how much money you have or are likely to have coming in,

2. Know how much money you have going out.

3. Make a plan for what to do with the difference, as long as it is positive, or how to cover the shortfall if it's not.

It doesn't matter which book you use, or which online website, which guru advises you or which relative with good fiscal sense finally talks some into you. If you can get these three points sorted out, and know what spare cash (if any) you have available, then life will be a lot easier.

And if there's no spare cash at all available? Welcome to my world. You are going to have to be one of the most creative people around, because you really are going to make magic from nothing. Just don't despair. If you are in really deep trouble, there are places to help you, and I'd advise you to visit them and get sorted straight away.

Now then, are you sorted? Got a budget set up that you are happy with? Excellent. If you can earmark a small amount for yourself every week as 'pocket money', that's a cute thing. If you can afford £5, the price of a magazine or a cheap Kindle book, that's a good start. Knowing that it's there and that you can have it if you want will give you a feeling of abundance that helps you to relax and enjoy living even more.

Try not to spend it every week, as well. Part of feeling happy is feeling self-sufficient, so we are going to see how happy we can be without a massive spending splurge. There will be books, treats, courses and items that you want to buy later on... but don't race out to get them now. Your new mantra for spending is quality, not quantity. Save the treat fund up, spend it on a night out, a good book, a craft course, whatever you like. It's your treat fund.

In my year of living hyggely I found that saving up my budgeted pocket money and then spending it on something I really wanted to do or had lusted after for a while gave me the best bang for my buck. It's the principle of delayed gratification. I like having a lust list in my planner, with the books, DVDs, clothes and events I want to experience on it. The waiting made the pleasure on achieving it even sweeter.

Action:

❖ Take a good look at your finances. Use a budgeting app or old-fashioned paper and pen to keep account of your finances.

❖ Start a lust list of things you want. You will find after a few weeks that you can tell which things you really want and which are passing fads.

❖ Borrow a good book on finance from the library. I like *The Debt Free Spending Plan* by Joanneh Naegler a lot, but that can be hard to get hold of. I have also found Mrs Moneypenny gives a lot of sensible advice in her book, *Financial Advice for Independent Women.* Others have told me that any book by Dave Ramsey will help sort out a spendthrift lifestyle. And good money advice is always available on www.moneysupermarket.com

Home decor puts function before form... but form needs to be good as well

When hygge made it big in 2016, the most commonly said thing about it was that it was a "Danish Interiors Trend". Images of cashmere-covered models' legs on faux fur throws and artistically crumpled grey linen sheets abounded, while a hygge living room was one that had a wood-burning stove, a classic Arne Jacobsen egg chair and white walls.

In other words, it was scandi-chic, and expensive to boot.

Now, my legs have never looked good in knee high socks, even when I was a little girl. I itch with too much linen and white walls... gah! They show up dirt, dust and soot like nothing else. And besides, I love colour.

But the chair.... Now, that I could understand. The classic egg chair is leather so it's hard wearing, but soft leather, so it's comfortable. It's shaped to allow a person to sit up, slouch, drape or sit cross-legged, so it's built for comfort. And although the price tag of a real Jacobsen chair is way beyond anybody I know, the right chair at the right price should be doable... shouldn't it?

The Arne Jacobsen chair is a prime example of form following function. At its heart, it is just a chair, but it has been designed so well that it would sit happily in a wide variety of ages, styles and rooms. A battered old egg chair will age with a patina and elegance that would make it more at home in a cosy library, a sparkling red chair would add colour to a minimalist flat in an instant.

My house is neither minimalist nor modern, so my chairs follow a different brief. They are comfortable, large enough for my sons (both over 6-foot tall) to sit in comfortably, covered in hard-wearing material, and came to us at the right price (mostly free, as part of an inheritance from a relative. Did I mention they are over 50 years old and still going strong?) I object to paying for furniture if I can get just as good for little or no price. I chose my style to be charity shop chic, so I'm happy to have dark wood furniture, crochet throws to cover any bald spots on the back of the settee and a colour scheme that was never in fashion, ergo can never actually be out of fashion. I don't do white, and I don't do magnolia.

In the past year I have bought two comfortable chairs from the local charity shops: one is a red Granny chair for the living room, but the other is a squishy, squashy black leather chair for the Hygge Nook (yes, I have a whole room in my house called the Hygge Nook) and it is delicious. Piled with cushions and throws, it's a warm hug of a chair for a cold, cold night.

Your home is just that: your home. At its most basic, the only people it needs to suit are you and your family. It needn't look good, needn't be a minimalist dream, unless that's your style, needn't have or do anything except that which suits you. Be selective: never buy anything on looks alone, and never spend full price if you can get it for less. Don't be tempted into the must-haves of the season unless it suits your style, and always buy classic rather than latest fad. By the time you reach middle age, you should know what suits you in home furnishings as well as fashionable clothes, so don't be afraid to say no to the latest things. Ikea's 1997 Chuck Out Your Chintz ad being a case in point. That year the Swedish furniture giant encouraged you to chuck out anything old fashioned or twee…. Within a few years, their biggest seller in the bed department was a bedspread called Rosali that looked a lot like… chintz. If you like pattern, go for pattern even in a monochrome year. If you love zebra stripe, get the stripes out even if nobody else has them. I would hate for my house to be dated by the décor. Like I say, never knowingly in fashion means I am never unknowingly out of fashion.

Action:

❖ Take a good look at your home. Does it have everything you need it to? Perhaps you need a desk to work at, but you've always wanted an old-fashioned bureau. Your curtains are getting threadbare and you'd love shutters at the window instead. Put them on your lust list and expect that the right objects at the right price will be yours at time not specified.

❖ *Flea Market Style* is a book by Emily Chalmers that is, sadly, out of print but shows how thrifted and acquired items can furnish a home with style and comfort.

❖ *A Sense of Home* by Helen James is subtitled Eat-Make-Sleep-Live. It's full of practical advice for making your house into a home that suits you, using all your senses.

Sanctuary. Create a nest that suits you.

My home (like I said) has a comfortable chair with a throw on it, ready to pull over my knees if they get cold. By the side there's a basket with a couple of my favourite magazines, my journal, some writing paper, a small pouch with hand cream, paracetamol and lip balm, another small pouch with a piece of embroidery that I can pick up, work on and drop down at a moment's notice, and an emergency bar of chocolate. The chocolate is the only thing that needs replacing often.

The chair is lit by a lamp that shines bright enough to read or sew by, while a table and coaster stand nearby ready for my cup of something warm and cosy. I have a good view of the TV, a good view of my family when they are all sat in the living room and a great view of the guinea pigs as they race around our floor at night. It's my sanctuary, and on a cold, wet, winter's night at work when I am waiting for the time to slip by ever so slowly, it is the place I long to be.

We all need a sanctuary, a safe place in our lives both physically and mentally. My chair gives me the physical comfort I need. Of course, it needn't have been my chair. In my teenage years my whole bedroom was very much my sanctuary, the place where I retreated when the world got too much. It was a place where I could be me, with no judgements, no eyes. In Danish it would be called a hyggekrog, a hygge nook or corner where you feel safe, comfortable. Cosy.

Start thinking now where your hygge nook might be. Is it a chair? The kitchen table? Your bed? You may be lucky enough to have all three as a hygge nook, in which case well done you.

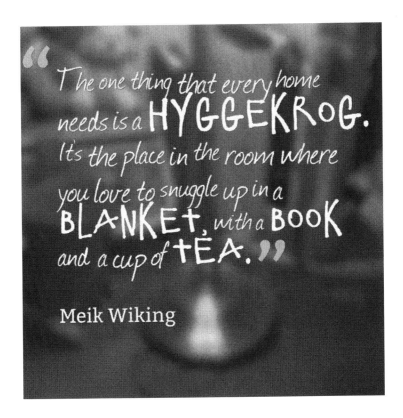

"The one thing that every home needs is a **HYGGEKROG.** It's the place in the room where you love to snuggle up in a **BLANKEt,** *with a* **BOOK** and a cup of **tEA.**"

Meik Wiking

Look closely at the corner you have chosen and think carefully: does it need anything else to make it even better? A throw, cushions, a candle. Perhaps you have no place to put your magazines or latest book? Is the lighting good enough there? You want it bright enough to read or work by, but not too bright.

Don't forget the nearby walls in your nook. Is there space for pictures or photographs? A noticeboard to hold postcards or souvenir photos, a map of your favourite city, or a picture that speaks to your heart can all be useful in a hygge nook.

When creating your sanctuary, try to engage all the senses. Have the pictures that suit, have access to music or sounds that soothe, use a scented candle or oil diffuser to spread restful scents around. Is the chair comfortable to touch? Do you need a softer throw? Make a note of the things you feel you need in your notebook. You may, or may not, want to buy them later, or you may find that the quilt you had in another room actually is the quilt you needed to complete your area. In other words, shop your house first before you look elsewhere.

Action:

❖ Collect what you need together. Look out for a container that suits your style. It might be that the box you've always used for the spare toilet rolls actually suits this purpose better, or you have an old suitcase that you bought on a whim that is ready and waiting to make your sanctuary complete.

❖ Make sure the rest of the house know this is 'your' space. Expect them to respect your space (but pay them back by respecting their space as well)

❖ There is a really useful description of an emergency hygge kit in *The Little Book of Hygge* by Meik Wiking. This is a lovely book for anyone who loves hygge to read.

❖ Read the lyrics to My House from the musical Matilda, written by Tim Minchin. It isn't much, but it is enough for me. There's your sanctuary for you.

This roof keeps me dry when the rain falls.
This door helps to keep the cold at bay.
On this floor I can stand on my own two feet.

On this chair I can write my lessons.
On this pillow I can dream my nights away.
And this table, as you can see, well, it's perfect for tea.

It isn't much but it is enough for me.
It isn't much but it is enough...

On these walls I hang wonderful pictures.
Through this window I can watch the seasons change.
By this lamp I can read, and I, I am set free!

And when it's cold outside I feel no fear!

Even in the winter storms, I am warmed by a small but stubborn

fire.

And there is no-where I would rather be.

Light therapy: Use your lighting options to best advantage.

In our homes, we have so many options for lighting available. Ask yourself: do you work best in sunlight, in dappled shade, with candles, overhead lighting, lamps casting pools of golden light on the floor, or a fluorescent tube that clicks when you turn it on?

Actually, that's a trick question. All the lighting options work well in different situations, except perhaps for the fluorescent tube that doesn't even work well as a budget lighting option in a workplace.

I found my obsession with candles when I first started living hyggely was wonderful. Every night I lined up my tealights in sparkling glasses, lit the fairy lights that decorated my fire and turned on the side lamps that have golden yellow bulbs. It does make for a relaxing environment, but the downside was that my guinea pigs got one chest infection after another, the fairy lights in the fireplace got chewed through and the side lamps needed their shades cleaning more often to help them to cast enough light to crochet by.

Now I (resignedly) choose to have fairy lights along my fireplace and lining my shelves instead of candles, and the fireplace sits waiting for my next big idea. I do have battery operated fairy lights wrapped around candles inside hurricane jars on either side of the fireplace. Is it authentically Danish Hygge? No, but it is British Pragmatic Hygge, which is all I ever profess to practise. If you want Danish hygge, go to Denmark.

The human body is very finely tuned, and responds to light whether there is too much or not enough of it. Recent research has shown that the blue light emitted by phones and tablets can have a detrimental effect on our sleeping rhythms[2]. Likewise, the lack of light in winter time has been linked to a rise in low feelings then that now has a proper name: Seasonal Affective Disorder. We do respond to the seasons and the natural light levels, we are hardwired to. What we need to do is to have the option available to keep ourselves in balance.

Think through your lighting. Use incandescent rather than LED bulbs in places where you want to relax, limit your screen time immediately before bed and try to have your evening lighting as soft as an arrangement of candles would be. Use table lamps rather than an overhead light or spotlights and use candles if you can to give the warm, yellow lighting you're after. I stop using my computer at nine pm if I'm not too busy. I check my phone once before bedtime, and my Kindle is a paperwhite, so it doesn't emit blue light.

If your lighting now is no good, but you can't afford to replace it all in one go, then make a bargain with yourself that you will replace the bulbs in your living room and bedroom with softer-lighting bulbs as and when they blow. And think laterally: have you got some Christmas fairy lights that you could put up instead, or display in a hurricane vase? You're looking for soft, golden, peaceful lighting that will create a relaxing feel, ready for bed.

Action:

❖ Don't be afraid to move lighting around until you find what suits you. Once I had found a solution that suited me and the guinea pigs, I was happier.

❖ Use lighting to make sleep and rest easier. Ban phones from the bedroom, put a curfew on computer use and try to have only soft lighting at night.

[2] https://www.nytimes.com/2017/02/10/realestate/light-bulbs-that-help-you-sleep.html

❖ Wake to natural daylight when it's the right time of year. There are few things more contentment creating than seeing the sun peep over the windowsill and hearing the birds singing. Only not at 4am. 6 or 7am is better.

What sparks joy for you? Do a William Morris in your house.

William Morris was a 19th Century British Artist and founder of the Arts and Crafts Movement. He believed in craftsmanship, and in having a home that suited you. His best-known saying? "Have nothing in your house that you do not know to be useful, or believe to be beautiful."

Since 2011, the modern version of this mantra has been to keep only those things which 'Spark Joy', as described in the book, *The Life Changing Magic of Tidying Up* by Marie Kondo. I love this book, although there are issues with it, as neatly illustrated in the joke, "I Konmari-ed the house, to get rid of everything that didn't spark joy, and threw out all my bras and my husband. I'm left with the dog and a packet of chocolate. What do I do now?"

I aim to keep the things in my house that spark joy (in Morris terms, these are the *'believe to be beautiful'* things) with the understanding that I may personally find joy in a lot of things at the moment, while a more minimalist-orientated person will find joy in only a few. When I started on my year's search to find happiness, I kept finding a lot of people who equated hygge with minimalism. I can't do that straight away. Being happy, for me, relies on having the things and people around me that I love.

It also relies on you being selective about those people and things. You don't, for example, need three can openers in your life, when you can have one really well-designed one that works. You don't need ten books on hygge, when three carefully chosen ones will give you the hygge hit you are looking for. You don't need to be out every night of the week with a different friend every time, when a night out once a week with your two best friends will give you the support and validation you need and let you be ready for work the next morning.

Sparking Joy is about recognizing your own needs in furniture, belongings and life, and choosing quality above quantity… but the style of that quality, and the criteria you judge it by are yours, rather than the rest of the worlds.

As the year has rolled by, and I have grown in happiness and self-confidence, I find I need less stuff. I trust my own style more, I am more selective about what I have in the house. I suppose I have moved further along the minimalist mindset, but only a little. I have learned to release people and objects without regret and with a whispered prayer of hope that they can make someone else happy. It takes effort, and time, but spending time to have a whole house that sparks joy in me, that I know to be useful and believe to be beautiful? That's time well spent.

Action:

- ❖ Get rid of duplicates that you don't need. Sort out things like the cutlery drawer and the pen pot regularly so that the stuff in it works, and you will find that little things make a difference over the year.
- ❖ Get used to asking yourself if an item sparks joy. Hold it, look at it, and learn to lose it.
- ❖ Not sure how to tell? Read *The Life Changing Magic of Tidying Up* and *Spark Joy*, both by Marie Kondo. She explains carefully how she can tell what is to keep and what is not.
- ❖ My three top hygge books? *The Little Book of Hygge* by Meik Wiking, *The Essence of Hygge* by Bronte Aurell and *The Book of Hygge* by Louisa Thomsen Brits. Oh, and my own books of course.

Love the House you have.

Are you moving soon? Can you afford to change anything big? Then you have to love the house you have. It is easy to spend hours on Zoopla or other house-selling sites looking for the 'perfect home' of your dreams. It's a bit like looking at other men in the pub when you are already married, though. You have a house and this is the one you're stuck with for the moment. Unless you intend to move (and even if you do) then this is the place where you need to concentrate your attention and create a home that encourages cosiness and contentment.

I found the book, *Love the Home You Have* by Melissa Michaels very useful. It's a book about making the most of what you have right now. It's about learning to love your home and let go of unrealistic expectations (you will never have the house out of Home Alone/It's Complicated/Practical Magic so give up on it now) and accepting the home you have now. I think that word is the key: home. The bricks and mortar you live in now make your home, so accept that and make it a proper home. I have always preferred the term 'homemaker' to 'housewife', because it allows for a degree of imperfection. You can have show houses, but never show homes because a home is a lived in, loved in place.

When I was reading every article available on hygge in 2016, I found that so many were actually advertorial copy put out by interior stores and retailers. They were about the style, the clean lines, the throws. I didn't find my happy home there. It was online, in Facebook and the glimpse into other people's homes on the blogs that I followed, where I found my homemaking heroes. In the little snippets of life and home I read, I saw things that I could do very easily to create a warmer, cosier home. Clearing the toy room and claiming it as a hygge nook, adding throws to all the seats, keeping the study ready for reading or working or web-surfing. Making sure there was always tea and coffee in the house, keeping a jar of biscuits for the teenage munchies. They are small actions, but they create a home much more than a big extension or grand house move would do.

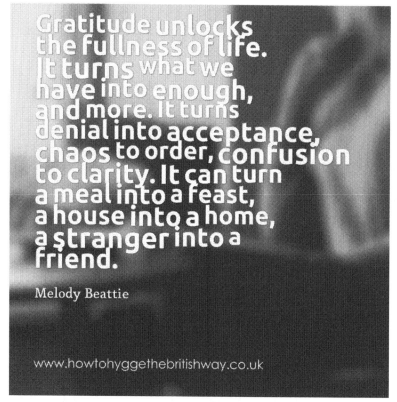

Gratitude unlocks the fullness of life. It turns what we have into enough, and more. It turns denial into acceptance, chaos to order, confusion to clarity. It can turn a meal into a feast, a house into a home, a stranger into a friend.

Melody Beattie

www.howtohyggethebritishway.co.uk

Be grateful for the place you call home. Whether it's an always home or a temporary accommodation, if you have a roof over your head and a bed to sleep in, then you are better off than most people in the world today. Accept that, imperfect as it may be, it's home, and breathe a prayer of thanks. Gratitude is a powerful force.

Action:

* Walk around your home and make a list of the things you love about it. Perhaps it has an old fireplace you love but make little of? Perhaps a window looks out onto a view that you love, even if it's the backyard with a pile of artistically arranged pots. Identifying the things that please you and give you a greater sense of homeliness.

* Add the touches you need to make a home. This will be personal for you, so think it through. Do you like biscuits? A bowl of fruit? Scented candles or unscented? *Love the Home You Have* has a 31 day Love Your Home challenge, a list of small(ish) things to encourage you to get your home to a state where you can love it.

* This sounds crazy, but it works. Stop talking your house down. Negative thoughts are more powerful than positive thoughts in a ratio of 5 to 1. In other words, you need 5 positive thoughts to balance out every negative thought. That's a lot of good thoughts needed to even out a bad vibe. At the very least phrase your thoughts positively. Instead of saying "I hate my sink: it's too small and splashes." Say "The sink is challenging, but it means I have to keep my concentration, which is a good skill for me to have". It will help you keep calm until you eventually get the money/time/inclination to change the problem.

Plan for the House you want.

Having said you're stuck with the house you have, so you have to love it, why not be aspirational as well? It's easy to start planning what your perfect house would look like, especially with the glut of house magazines available and the masses of images and ideas available on Pinterest. Often, identifying and curating an ideal room will give you ideas for improving the home you have.

I love spending time on Pinterest, especially since it has such a vast range of ideas all available at the press of a mouse button. For the past few years, I don't think I've celebrated a Christmas, decorated a room or contemplated a holiday away without starting a Pinterest board for it. My bedroom, kitchen, hall and family room have all had aspirational pinboards started. Just scrolling through pictures of, say, blue walls or coat storage or spice organization has helped me to identify the small improvements that I can make now and to recognise the big things that I'd be looking for in a new house/kitchen/whatever when the time comes.

In *Simple Abundance* by Sarah Ban Breathnach (how I love that book!) she advocates the use of an Illustrated Discovery Journal to collect the images, quotes and ideas that speak to you. I think Pinterest is something similar in electronic form. Through pinning pictures and articles for the past few years, I have discovered that I love colour, adore red and white as Christmas colours, will always save a picture with a lady in boots (I adore boots) and that my ideal home is so eclectic that it evades any sort of theme or style name imposed on it.

Of course, if I pinned every pin with the intention of doing them, I would drive myself mad. I know when I pin them that they're there for inspiration not as a to-do list. Just last autumn, I went through my older boards and found out that some of the pins were no longer what I wanted or needed. I edited them out, rearranged the boards to suit me, and kept on pinning. Collect, collate, refine, repeat.

Action:

❖ Set up your Pinterest boards and be prepared to use them. Pin a lot of pictures that catch your attention, sort them out into boards according to interest and keep looking over them. You will see your styles probably change over the years, sometimes radically, other times only by a little amount.

❖ If you love paper, then be old-fashioned and keep a book that you stick pictures and articles in. It's not as easy to edit, but it's still good stimulation for your creative side.

❖ Ask yourself if any of the ideas for your perfect home can be implemented now? Perhaps you don't have a fireplace, but could use a shelf on the wall as a replacement mantelpiece until you do? Or your porch-free front door could be made better with the addition of a small cupboard next to it to store wellies and umbrellas.

Happiness At Home Resources

Websites and Articles

http://www.telegraph.co.uk/women/womens-business/9566120/Arguing-about-money-How-to-stop-falling-out-over-financial-problems.html

http://www.apa.org/helpcenter/money-conflict.aspx

https://www.cnbc.com/2015/02/04/money-is-the-leading-cause-of-stress-in-relationships.html Money causes massive issues in a relationship.

https://howtohyggethebritishway.com/2017/09/07/creating-a-comfortable-space-wherever-you-are/ How I used what I had to create my comfort basket next to my chair.

https://www.nytimes.com/2017/02/10/realestate/light-bulbs-that-help-you-sleep.html

Books

Financial Advice for Independent Women by Mrs Moneypenny and Heather McGregor

The Debt Free Spending Plan by Joanneh Naegler

Flea Market Style by Emily Chalmers and Debbie Treloar. Sadly out of print. It's home décor on a budget, and sourced from charity, rummage and yard sales.

A Sense of Home by Helen James. I love the simplicity of the book, its mix of interior design and cooking, and the colours she uses in her own home.

The Life Changing Magic of Tidying Up and Spark Joy by Marie Kondo. Time well spent in a house. If you learn nothing else, take the tip about folding t shirts in a drawer and run with it.

The Little Book of Hygge by Meik Wiking. The book credited with introducing hygge to the world, it's a pretty, easy and eye-catching book filled with ideas and inspiration for making life more cozy.

The Essence of Hygge by Brontë Aurell. Part hygge guide, part recipe book, this is a beautiful small volume that has photos to look at forever. One of my favourites.

The Book of Hygge by Louisa Thomsen Brits. This is a why to rather than a how to. It has no illustrations and is quite text-heavy, but it is full of inspirational quotes.

Love The Home You Have by Melissa Michaels. Look at the home you are living in, love it and make it work for you. I love the 31-day love your home challenge.

Happiness with Your Daily Life

Life is just so daily... it starts and it goes on and on... And because we have to live our own lives, rather than permanently escape into an alternate universe, it's worth sorting out our daily life so that it functions well and supports us in our quest for happiness.

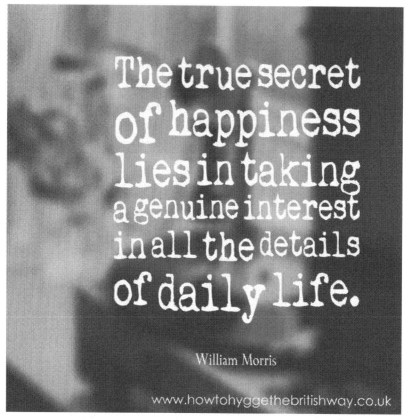

The true secret of happiness lies in taking a genuine interest in all the details of daily life.

William Morris

www.howtohyggethebritishway.co.uk

Looking at the support systems you have in place, the things you spend time, effort and emotion on, the small details of your daily life, makes you focus on the things that you have set as a priority. If you spend all your energy on work and don't have enough energy to spend with family and friends, then you have got your priorities skewiff.

In the words of the old saying, nobody ever looked back at their life from their deathbed and wished they'd spent more time at work. Take some time and get your daily life in balance, with planning tools, support systems and relationships for maximum health and happiness.

Friends make life worthwhile.

In all the various ways to be happy, spending time with other people you love and trust has to be the number one choice. For a lot of people, that's their family, but it's important even when you're knee deep in nappies and busy clearing up after children to keep in touch with a few people who make you smile, make you cry, keep you sane and show you that you are not alone. Yes, that's your friends. When my children were little, I found it easy to steer them towards suitable friendships (suitable to my way of thinking, that is). Now I watch the three young adults go out of the house and listen to who they're hanging out with and have no say on their friendships. I have to trust that they will recognise the positive and the poisonous themselves and be strong enough to keep one and jettison the other.

In *Friendfluence*, Carlin Flora argues that our friends play a crucial role in making us who we are. They help us to set our boundaries, to refine our life priorities, and to shape our viewpoints on most areas of living. Sometimes they can limit us, if all our friends come from the same gender/ethnicity/religion/fandom as we do. During the US election and Brexit in the UK the idea of 'bubbles' of thought on social media pointed out the problems with never meeting views different to your own.

Who we work to be friends with says a lot about who we are. Do we have a bunch of bitchy, gossipy, back-biting friends? That's not good. Do we have happy friends who keep us happy? Friends in need who we support, and who support us back? Friends from different social, educational and interest backgrounds? I like having a variety of friends, some real, some online. I hope I'm a good friend who could be called on in a crisis, or for a good idea for something to do. I know when I look back at my times of crises, the people who were often there for me were my friends. At times of crises for the whole family, for example bereavement, it can be hard to share your true emotions with family who may be drowning in sorrow themselves, while a friend who is slightly more detached from the loss will be better placed to provide empathy and support.

And friendship gets more important as we age. People who reported stronger, more supportive friendships in older age were likely to be happier and healthier in a recent report in the USA[3].

Over the past year of happiness, I've found spending time with friends has played a big part in my happiness. Some of my friends have been met through groups like the Women's Institute, others are friends from different stages of life. Meeting up with them, sharing a good time chatting or drinking or just hanging about has made me happier. I don't have many close friends, but those I do have mean a lot to me.

And I found an online tribe: The Hygge Nook group on Facebook was a group I set up to find people who loved the relaxed, comfortable security of the hygge mindset and were looking to get more into their life. I'd like to think I can count several of the members as

---

[3] http://time.com/4809325/friends-friendship-health-family/

virtual friends as well. Certainly, they are quick to offer emotional support and advice when I seek it. And for that, I'm very grateful.

Action:

* Set up regular friendship sessions and keep to them. If you can't justify a night a month just sitting drinking sparkly white wine and talking….well. You don't need to justify it at all. Call it a Mental Health Evening.

* If you're lacking in friends and want to find some more, try joining a society built around your interests, or a general society such as the Women's Institute, The Rotary Club or campaigning groups. Finding people with similar interests helps when building a new friendship.

* If you live in an isolated place, why not build friendships online? Join a few groups on Facebook in areas you like. Crafters will often find there's a group set up for a knit-a-long or crochet-a-long project. Sharing little and often is a good way to meet others who like what you like, and then you can become Facebook friends, pen-friends and eventually proper friends. It takes time, and you get out of a virtual group what you put in, so don't sit there and expect the friends to jump into your lap. You are going to have to post regularly, share feelings (although be careful what personal information you share for internet safety, obviously) and be prepared to keep sharing.

* There isn't a group organised around your interests? Start one. Find a convenient café, post a few notices and hold the first meeting. And the second. And the third. It takes time to get anything off the ground, so be prepared to start very slowly.

Plan Your Daily Life

Planning and hygge? Do they go together? Isn't hygge a free-spirited, freedom-loving thing that can't be timetabled and won't come when you pencil it in? Well, to an extent, yes.

Which is why you need to plan the rest of your life well enough to give you the time, freedom and space you need to enjoy living.

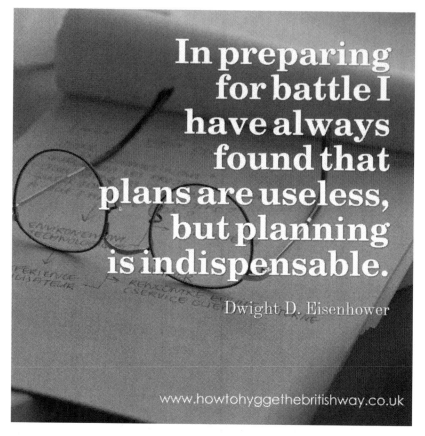

In preparing for battle I have always found that plans are useless, but planning is indispensable.

Dwight D. Eisenhower

www.howtohyggethebritishway.co.uk

I found that my time at work could very easily swallow up all my time. It's Parkinson's Law, you see. Work expands to fill the time allotted to it, and if you don't allot time to a project whether at work or home, and keep to it, the project expands to fill all previously unallocated time. Added to that the fact that I work in our family business, that the work I was doing was new to me at first and we (the Husband and I) were still working out the dynamics of office life together and work was a ravaging beast in the summer of 2016 that swallowed up all our free time and a lot of time that we should have given to the children.

When summer turned to Autumn, I had to reprioritize my life. I grabbed a book, got a pen and started planning. Allocating time for different activities, establishing a pattern to the week and sticking with it, setting aside time for crafts and hobbies and putting personal time with the teenage children and my husband at the top of my list helped me set a better pattern to my life.

I got more time-savvy at work. There are some excellent books on time management and project planning out there. I found both these books useful: *Getting Things Done* by David Allen, which lists actions by location, and *Eat That Frog!* by Brian Tracy which encourages us to do first the tasks we hate the most. You need to have a system that you trust and that you find easy to use. It has to be adaptable to suit your life, and to have the flexibility to accommodate your needs. You might need to trial a planning style for a few weeks before making up your mind whether it is too cumbersome, too lightweight or too much writing for you.

My time planning now runs on keeping a calendar up to date with all my commitments, having action lists for work, home and blog and marking in my free time as actual commitments. I need my evenings and weekends at home doing nothing: I'm not a 24/7 activity person.

I keep well-organised at work, and have lists of actions I need to do, and while at work I work hard. There's not a lot of idle chatter between the two of us, but we do take coffee breaks and lunchtime together is sacrosanct. And when I get home.... Well. That time is mine to do with as I wish. I feel more productive, but I also know I need to be relaxed. Being well-organised lets me achieve that.

Action:

- ❖ Find the time management system that works for you. The internet has lots of ideas on how to use your time, whether you are a professional or not. If housekeeping is your bugbear, then Flylady.com is a popular site which, if followed absolutely, will give you a clean home with a fair bit of effort. It probably won't suit working people, so read, adapt and do what you can.

- ❖ Even creative people need some sort of timetable or planning. Try to establish a pattern to the week, but keep it flexible. Call it a life skeleton, if you're truly allergic to the idea of a timetable. Life works much better when the routine events happen automatically and leave your time and brain-power free to think about other stuff.

Take your time back. You do not owe anything to anyone else once you leave your desk. Bronte Aurell
www.howtohyggethebritishway.com

❖ Learn to say no. Your work does not deserve your whole life, so set limits and stick to them. The same is true of that needy friend or relative. You are entitled to time just for you. A firm but friendly no is a useful tool in your armory. You don't even need to give a reason why. Just say no.

My Planner: Paper vs Digital

Whichever system or planning rules of whichever book appeals or suits your lifestyle, you will need to keep track of it. Your first question has to be: paper or digital?

It's a funny thing, how much time we spend planning our lives. We so convince ourselves of what we want to do, that sometimes we don't see what we're meant to do."

Susan Gregg Gilmore

Paper planners come in many shapes and sizes, so it's worth looking around for one that suits you. There's a choice between ringed planners (for example, Filofax or Kikki-K) and bound planners with ring-binding or flat edging, notebooks with plain, lined or grid paper and whether you want to use pencil, pen or fountain pen in the planner. The relative benefits or drawbacks of each one can be found by looking online or in a planner group on Facebook. Believe me, I've tried them all and ultimately there isn't a lot to choose between them. Just don't switch between different sorts too often or you'll find any planning time taken up with writing out your diary for the third time that month... and life can be just as well-planned in an ordinary exercise book from the corner shop.

I have a real dichotomy about paper planners. I love the idea of a beautiful, pretty planner with washi tape, pen and ink drawings and colour washes decorating the diary pages, but I need my planner to be a practical thing, full of scribbles and errors that I have corrected over the weeks. I don't want to give over a lot of time to decorating what is essentially (for me) a tool, so I keep it plain and ignore any scribbles or mistakes I make. If you want to see beautiful planners, may I suggest you type "Bullet Journal" into Pinterest and scroll down. Just don't do it when you've only got a few minutes, as they will suck you in. Boho.Berry on Instagram also posts some beautiful pages. And the original introduction to Bullet Journals can be found on bulletjournal.com.

For me, the practical wins out. I use either a ring bound planner or a dotted notebook, depending on my mood. I tend to keep the same lists in both, and just update as needed. I like a ring-bound for the versatility, since when I need to update a list it's a simple matter of ripping a page out and starting again, but the notebooks have a definite weight advantage, as well as encouraging me to accept life as a real mess, which I need to do now and again as well.

During my year long search for happiness, I found the notebooks gave me space for one of my other favourite things: collecting inspirational quotes. Because of how the Bullet Journal system works, I could see a quote I liked, write it down and use it later in my writing, as long as I had entered it in the contents.

Now is a good time to come clean and say that whichever paper system I use, I keep an online digital back-up. There are apps and to do lists galore available, but I love to use Evernote. Seriously, it covers all my needs. I can access it from all my electrical devices, add notes, store them and search them. I have the Premium paid version now, for business reasons, but the basic free version has most of the functions you need initially, including letting you keep your notes in Notebooks according to subject and sharing files with others. I think the same functions are also available in Google Drive and Microsoft One Note, but I like the user interface of Evernote, as well as the archive system. A useful book here is

Master Evernote: An unofficial guide to organising your life with Evernote by S.J. Scott, which has all the advice and ideas you'd need to get good at searching, organising and keeping your life sorted. I even have a fair selection of my recipes uploaded to Evernote ready for holidays or meal planning.

I did, for one brief, horrible winter, try using only a digital planner. Using Google Calendar and Evernote together, I tried to do without paper altogether. I missed the writing, and the chance to see the corrections I had made. I also discovered that paper (whichever system you use) doesn't need batteries. I found it was Sod's Law that the phone or tablet would die in the middle of me recording an important date, and I'd end up needing a paper reminder anyway. Plus, checking for dates and tasks in the week ahead wasn't as much fun on a digital system for me. That's not to say you won't enjoy it.

I'm happiest planning on paper, but happier with a digital back up. Does that make sense? No, but it doesn't have to. It suits me and, ultimately in happy planning, that's all it has to do.

Action:

❖ What's your preferred planner? Paper or digital? Ring bound or notebook? If you have one you're happy with, that's great. If not, read a few articles about planning online and give one a go. The Bullet Journal system can be done in any paper planner, so buy a cheap notebook and give it a go.

❖ Entry level ring-bound systems can be bought for as little as £15 if you buy a Filofax Clipbook. Be warned, the ring-bound world is full of attractive binders that you may fall in love with but never be able to afford. Be prepared to give yourself a good talking to and change the page when the temptation gets too much.

❖ Set up your planner and use it. Take a few minutes each evening to look at it ready for the next day, and a few more minutes on a Sunday night to plan for the week ahead, coordinate online and paper planner and get prepared.

Set a Goal and write it down.

At College, when I was training to teach, we used to have to write lesson plans for every lesson, and at the top of every plan we wrote the aims and objectives for the lesson. The aim was the big thing you wanted the children to gain at the end of the lesson, while the objectives were the little steps or the measurable achievements that you were working through.

I could set aims for the lesson brilliantly, since for English it was mostly 'learn to read' but I was always useless at setting the specific objectives for each lesson. I don't do micro detail. I like a big goal, like contentment, rather than a lot of little objectives. I still am a big picture girl.

When I started looking into hygge and Lagom, I found that a lot of the lifestyle goals that I saw around me struck me as hollow. What is the point of the biggest, fastest car in the world when mostly you're stuck doing 30 miles an hour? Why would I need exotic holidays to escape my life if I loved life itself? Do I really need to shop, shop, shop 'til I drop, drop, drop?

I thought over my life goals. I looked at my principles, and I tried to get them in alignment. Now my goals are easier, achievable, and a lot more relaxing.

I simply want to live in contentment with enough to live on for a reasonably simple lifestyle, friends to spend time with, a family to love and health to enjoy it.

I have that ambition written in my notebook, since writing your goals down is proven to make you more likely to achieve them. I also have my medium-term goals noted down: to write a book about planning for a Frugal Christmas, to clear the clutter from my house and to visit Denmark in the next few years.

And (despite having never been a micro-goal person) I also have the next steps I need to do to achieve them written on my to do list. Just the next one step, then I'll think of the step beyond that. I am seeking to live in the here and now. To be able to take the opportunities that life gives me now, not to seek for the greater things that might be. In St Helens (near where I was born) there is a pub called Bird I'Th Hand. As in, a bird in the hand is worth two in the bush. Be content with what you have.

I am content;
that is a blessing
greater than riches;
and he to whom
that is given need
ask no more.

Henry Fielding

www.howtohyggethebritishway.co.uk

Action:

❖ What is your life goal? What do you really want from life? You don't have to plan every move you will make, indeed you shouldn't. But you should know the final destination you're aiming for. Do you want to be a writer? Work in nursing? Have a dog? Write them down, and see whether you move towards them.

❖ Set a few medium-term goals. Keep them **SMART**: **s**pecific, not wooly, **m**easurable so you know when you've achieved it, **a**ction-orientated, realistic and not beyond your abilities, and time-limited. If you don't achieve a goal within the time limit, you want to look at them and see if you still want to achieve them. Goals are not set in stone, nor are they the be-all and end-all of life. You should never focus on your goals so much that you ignore the opportunity under your feet.

Just do it.

But what do you do when an opportunity does come along? One that is too good to miss? Well, if you can afford it, if it really makes you feel good and it's not too dangerous.... Just do it.

Life is for living, after all, and contentment will carry us only so far. At a certain point in life you have to grab it by the throat and live with passion. If you are always concentrating on the Big Picture and the goals along the way, you run the risk of missing out on opportunity. Having the wisdom to know when to set aside a goal and act on impulse is the hard part. I found *Big Magic* by Elizabeth Gilbert helped me a lot. In this book, she explains that we don't have to jump at every chance the Universe presents, since the Universe will throw out the same invitation to a lot of people. She tells the story of an idea she had for a novel, but never got far on due to lack of commitment, only to find that the same or similar idea had been taken to completion by another novelist. You can see a similar idea in effect when two or more movies or TV series come out along the same lines... Think of 1991, when Kevin Costner and Patrick Bergin both ended up playing Robin Hood in separate movies.

In fact, we need to recognise the opportunities that we need to answer as against the opportunities that are just there. I'd go with listening to your body here. Gut instinct is very good at letting us know when a thing feels right or not. Get good at listening out for the butterflies of excitement or the heavy feeling of dread. A project that inspires you will feel like no burden, even if you are spending a ridiculous amount of time on it, so as far as possible try to choose the jobs that give you this feeling. There should be a level of joy in creating that drives us along.

CREATE. NOT FOR THE MONEY. NOT FOR THE FAME. NOT FOR THE RECOGNITION. BUT FOR THE PURE JOY OF CREATING SOMETHING AND SHARING IT.

Ernest Barbaric

www.howtohyggethebritishway.co.uk

Action

- ❖ Say yes. Just do it.
- ❖ Always keep a notebook to list the things you may or may not want to do in the future. Keep editing the list, taking off those items that no longer spark creative joy in you, and putting on your new ideas.

Find your tribe.

That's not always your immediate family, although in many cases it will be. You're looking for the people who give you unconditional support, love, and understanding. The ones that appreciate your quirks or even share them with you.

I'm very lucky that my two teenage sons share the same or similar taste in films most of the time. They're happy to take me to see the latest DC or Marvel superhero film, to talk Shared Universe with me and even (the shame) to sit next to me during Deadpool for an 18th birthday treat (seriously, I was not meant to go, but someone pulled out at the last minute, and we'd booked the tickets. I offered to sit elsewhere in the cinema, but the tickets were numbered and the showing was fully booked. I had to sit at the end of the row with a gang of 18-year old boys and pretend I wasn't with them. Parents don't take their teenagers to see films like that... do they? Responsible parents don't. It was very rude, but oh, so funny). They're one of my tribes. I know that Thor, The Avengers, Justice League or whatever, they'll talk through the intricacies of the plot with me.

I also benefit from the virtual hygge tribe on Facebook. I belong to several hygge-based groups, but the one that gives me greatest pleasure is The Hygge Nook, the group I set up in October 2016 because I wanted a place where people who loved hygge could share their experiences. It keeps on growing, and has taken us all through a US Presidential election and a UK election with no politics, no arguments (mostly) and a commitment to friendship around the world. My blog has a Facebook page, but that wasn't conducive to letting everyone share stuff, so the Facebook group works better. I have a few friends from real life who joined the Hygge Nook and a few friends I've made since being on it that are always ready to offer good advice on different things.

Your tribe may be family or friends, live near you or live far away. What they should be is there when you need them, ready with emotional or actual support and brave enough to give you an honest answer. We are all human beings, and sometimes we get a bee in out bonnet about the wrong thing, a tweet that we have read in the wrong way, a comment that has been taken as one thing when it was meant as another and, often in my case, I am actually kicking off about something I can't change and I need a friend to tell me to stop, think about it and then either accept the situation or make a change. They have my back. I have theirs. Find a tribe.

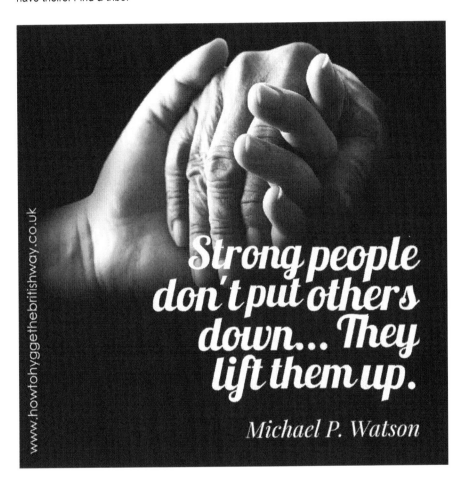

Strong people don't put others down... They lift them up.

Michael P. Watson

www.howtohyggethebritishway.co.uk

Action

❖ Find people that you enjoy spending time with. Build your relationship with them by spending time, real or virtual, together.

❖ Be a good friend. Offer to help others without expecting a return service. You never know when the little aid you do today will be paid back to you. The Universe has a great way of balancing out good actions. Call it Karma.

Spend time, not money, on people.

Which would you rather have, a massive present off a friend or an evening with that friend enjoying a chat and a drink together?

Would you rather have a book you'll never read or an hour's walk in the park with a parent?

Would you rather have another photo frame on an already crowded wall or a video evening with your children watching a movie that makes you all laugh?

My bet is you picked the experience over the present. Spending money on gifts and presents is easy, especially near Christmas when the papers are full of the things we need to buy that year. Yet very often the cost of the present is immaterial to the receiver. One study in 1993 estimated that the recipients surveyed underestimated the value of the presents received by as much as 10%, while the Money Advice Service worked out that the unwanted presents in the UK for Christmas 2014 alone was a staggering 2.4 million pounds. [4]

Happiness research, meanwhile, points out that spending money to free up time, not to accumulate stuff, makes us happier.[5] Rethink your present giving this year. If you live close enough, the gift of your own time can be a great present for a close friend or relative. Go walking, go skating, visit a zoo. Take your friend out for a meal or drinks, form a Dr Who Appreciation Society of two. Whatever, spend the time together and be happier than if you spent money.

Last Christmas I looked at my Mum and Dad, both in their 70s, both well and both keen to say that they needed nothing. No clothes, no books, nothing that would fill up their home any more than it already was filled. I offered them an afternoon a week, just to come and sit on their settee, or to go out for coffee, to the shops or whatever. I gave them a gift of time. It's only been a month, but already I look forward to my Tuesday afternoons. I have time to sit and talk, time to get to know my parents again without rushing to get somewhere else. When the good weather comes, we have plans to do. This Tuesday we're visiting

---

[44] https://www.themoneypages.com/latest-news/2-4-billion-spent-wasted-presents/

[55] http://www.bbc.co.uk/news/science-environment-40703519

Hobbycraft for material and thread for a present, next Tuesday we may visit a Garden centre. It really doesn't matter where we go, just that we go.

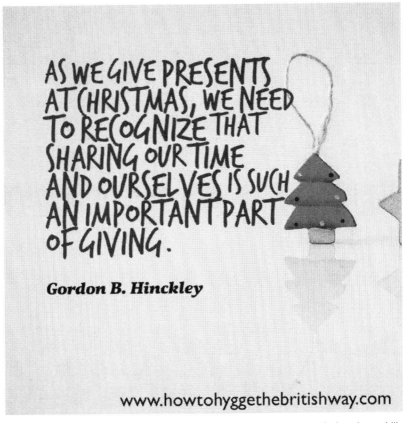

AS WE GIVE PRESENTS AT CHRISTMAS, WE NEED TO RECOGNIZE THAT SHARING OUR TIME AND OURSELVES IS SUCH AN IMPORTANT PART OF GIVING.

Gordon B. Hinckley

www.howtohyggethebritishway.com

Likewise with my children: we have most of the physical things we need already, so I like to treat them with experiences where possible. Family nights at the cinema, trips to the theatre and a much-anticipated trip to Chester Zoo (inspired by The Secret Life of the Zoo on Channel 4) build valuable bonding time into our lives and give us all a memorable experience. Shared memories to look back on when I am old and grey (so: next week then, as my daughter would reply)

Action

❖ Start to think differently about presents. They don't always come in a box. Make a list of experiences that would make good presents, such as cinema, shopping, theatre or wildlife parks.

❖ Experiences needn't cost a massive amount either. Be creative and have a themed afternoon or evening soiree. Run a casino party, with poker, roulette and Vingt-et-Un (Blackjack, or Twenty One). Have proper afternoon tea at home or in a hotel, have a mid-winter picnic with tomato soup and toasted cheese sandwiches or visit the local beach for a sandcastle making competition with friends. Be creative and use the internet for inspiration.

❖ Give long-lasting presents like a year's membership to a society or attraction.

❖ Never underestimate how valuable just having uninterrupted time with the members of your family can be. Having a chance to share their memories while they are still here could be the best present your parents give you this year.

Helping others helps you: altruism makes me happy

It's a proven fact that spending time and money helping other people will boost your happiness levels. It's a win-win situation: that afternoon in school volunteering to hear readers, the trip to the supermarket for the little old lady next door, spending an afternoon shopping for a special dress with your best friend. These are all ways both to boost your happiness and build your friendship bonds.

But helping others doesn't have to take up time or require you physically to be present. You can give money or goods to charities and reap the benefits of generosity as well. There is always a way to help others and thereby help yourself. Here are some of my favourite ways:

- Keep a change jar by the front door or your bedside table and put all your spare change into it every few days. When you've collected a fair amount, take it and put it in a charity box somewhere.

- Tick the 'make a donation' box that often appears at the bottom of, for example, a Hungry House order page. Every fifty pence adds up and helps a charity to help others.

- Add a couple of tins to every supermarket shop and give them to the local Foodbank. If your supermarket doesn't have a basket already out for donations, then either take them to your local church who will probably be collecting for the local foodbank all year round or make your donation virtual by setting up a monthly gift. Just a couple of pounds a month means that the organisers can buy the things that they need to give away that month, often toiletries and sanitary products that get overlooked.

When we give cheerfully and accept gratefully, everyone is blessed.

Maya Angelou

www.howtohyggethebritishway.co.uk

- Donate your time to a school, youth group or other organization. There will always be a local group in need of help. Be aware, you may need background checks or references to be accepted as a volunteer in most places.
- Use your skills well. Do you have a hobby or are you skilled in a craft? Sharing that in a social setting, and teaching others how to do it, benefits both teacher and pupil.

- Don't be shy about offering your professional skills as a volunteer either. Forbes magazine found that retired or semi-retired professionals felt using their skills to the max had a positive effect on their own professional life[6].

Let your brain think about things: you are bound to find the right opportunity for you somewhere.

Action:

❖ What have you got to offer? Do a time, money and skills audit to decide what you can afford both physically and mentally. It's no use volunteering in a school if you have no patience for it. Likewise, a very active volunteer post won't suit you if you're housebound.

❖ Start locally. Ask your family and friends for any opportunities or links they have. It's easier to offer and be accepted somewhere they have heard of you, or a family member, and where you both start with a level of trust.

❖ Nothing is too small. Can you only afford a couple of pounds now and again? Great: that makes the difference to whoever you give it to. Our smallest actions leave a big impression.

---

[6] https://www.forbes.com/sites/nextavenue/2016/05/11/how-to-find-the-ideal-place-to-volunteer/#42b740357c87

Happiness With Your Daily Life Resources

Websites and Articles

https://www.facebook.com/groups/TheHyggeNook This is the Facebook group I started up as a place for people to share the hygge in their everyday life. It's a lovely and very accepting place.

http://www.flylady.net/ The home blessing system is designed for people who have plenty of time to do the work, but it's a useful site for tips and ideas on establishing a home keeping routine.

http://bulletjournal.com/ Advice and guidance on setting up the latest and most adaptable planning system. It includes an introductory video that explains how to get started.

Books

Friendfluence: The Hidden Ways in Which Friendships Make Us Who We Are by Carlin Flora.

Getting Things Done by David Allen. This time-management book is a popular way to organise your life, especially amongst offices.

Eat That Frog! by Brian Tracy. Do the hard stuff first. Another classic time management book.

Master Evernote by S.J.Scott

Big Magic by Elizabeth Gilbert. I love Eat Pray Love as well. Inspiring ways to live.

Happiness in your own Body

How hard it is to accept that we are perfectly imperfect human beings! The current media pressure for perfect bodies seems to have us looking and comparing ourselves against the models and actors that advertise everything from make up to motorcars via almost every product in between. We can know and tell ourselves that the front cover of the magazines that we see everywhere are airbrushed to perfection and thus represent unattainable levels of beauty, but our inner reptile brain doesn't get that idea, and still puts us under pressure to look as good as that.

Learning to love yourself just as you are is the first step in building a better world. If you don't love yourself, hold yourself in esteem or trust yourself to do the best that you can do, how can you feel the same about anybody else? How can you trust that they love you, when your very body is telling you to question the reason why?

I found this chapter incredibly hard to write. For years I have battled with poor self-worth and a bad self-image. It was only when I actually did something extraordinary that I thought... one small step... if I can do that, then what else can I do? And I looked at my life in a different way. I began to list my positives, all the things I did automatically that were good, and looked at what I could do to be and feel better. Happiness may be an emotion, but there is a whole physical side to it that can help you to feel happier and stay content. My discoveries, as well as the advice I know is good but still haven't fully implemented, are in this collection of essays.

I hope this chapter will act as a catalyst for anyone who needs a reminder: you are perfect just as you are. You are worth knowing and loving, so get on with it and own your life.

You are perfect just the way you are

Why do we have such a hard time loving ourselves? We often seem prepared to overlook the faults in those we love, to take the sarcastic with the sweet or the forgetful moments with the ultimate in remembering our favourite ice cream flavours. We let others away with being themselves, human, flawed, wonderfully idiosyncratic, but we seem unable to look at ourselves through the same forgiving lens.

I bet in a meeting of any more than 2 women discussion will eventually turn to how fat/thin/tall/short/curly haired/funny-toothed one or other of them feels. It's like we've been trained from an early age to look at ourselves and not see a wonderful human being, a body that is a marvel of technical design in the way it moves, operates and especially thinks.

Are we daft, or what? If we let issues about ourselves, especially our appearance, have an impact on our sense of worth, then we are letting ourselves down.

The title of this section isn't actually right. We aren't perfect, of course we aren't, because nobody is. But we are good enough, whatever mental or physical state we are in. Capable of improvement? Yes, because everything in life is either getting better or getting worse. Stasis (going nowhere) is not a natural state of affairs, and not one we want to be aiming for. But accepting ourselves just the way we are while working on improving areas of our life that need improvement makes sense. We need to be able to accept our flaws as just us, so that as we do journey on through life we're spending time with someone we love, not somebody we despise.

Action

❖ Write a list of all the best bits about you, physically mentally or emotionally. It could be your hair, your smile, your ability to do sudoku. Whatever. Write the list and keep it close to hand in a notebook or planner. On those days when you are feeding your inner critic, hit back. Read the list and remember you are good enough just as you are. Repeat it to yourself every morning as you brush your teeth and every evening as you brush your hair.

❖ Read a book like What's Holding You Back by Sam Horn. This one has a 30 day programme, using quotations, questionnaires and quick sets of information to read, think about and implement. Often, the thing standing between you and achievement is.... You.

❖ Collect your favourite positive quotations and either write them out by hand or print off small colour versions to laminate and stick around the home or workplace. Imagine having one by the bathroom mirror and getting a burst of positivity when you brush your teeth. I love to use a simple app like www.quotescover.com for making mine.

Happy-proof Your Diet

Is there a worse time of year for contemplating dieting than January? The weather goes cold, the bills roll in, the sky is nowhere near the blue you want it to be for as long as you want it to be, and yet so many people figure that now is the time to constrict food and lose weight.

I swore off proper dieting the year I was writing How to Hygge. Somehow, writing about fika breaks (the Swedes have daily coffee breaks often accompanied by a sweet something) and about how being cosy can boost the mood wasn't conducive to turning my nose up at every treat that passed me by.

I also didn't want to put on any more weight than I had to, so I had to find a workable alternative. My hygge diet was born.

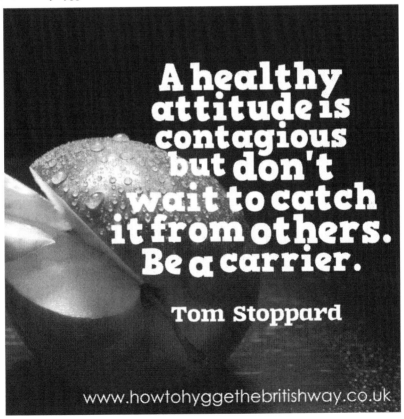

I eat well, but carefully. My basic rules for food are:

1. **Don't eat a lot of processed food.** The nearer the original thing something looks, the better. This means keeping away from too many packet food, pies, sausages or convenience meals. I cook most of our meals from scratch, and in my Absolute Domestic Goddess moments even make bread.

2. **Eat The Rainbow.** This means eating as many different coloured fruit and vegetables as I can get to. I love eating vegetables as soups or stews in the winter, and salads full of green in the summer.

3. **Make half the plate vegetables.** I cut back on carbs, because processed carbs make me feel ill, and bulk up my meals with vegetables. A plate of carrot and swede mash, with bacon and fried mushrooms is as good as a plate of pasta. I also love butternut squash drizzled with chilli oil, sprinkled with salt and roasted until soft in the middle and slightly crisped at the edges.

4. **Enjoy an occasional treat, but really enjoy it,** and don't just eat something because it's there. I have got more mindful about my treats. I sit for a few minutes before I go and get one and ask myself what do I fancy? What taste or feel or scent am I after? If I can't satisfy my inner want, then I am better off not having anything/ I would rather wait for a proper egg custard, top thickly dusted with nutmeg, for example than have just any old cake. Likewise, I have trained myself to appreciate good quality chocolate eaten in small squares rather than any old supermarket chocolate. Mindless eating is no good for anyone.

Two books I have found useful are *The Happy Kitchen* by Rachel Kelly and *The Dopamine Diet* by Tom Kerridge. Both aim to use food to boost mood, keeping you happier and encouraging a balanced attitude to life. Rachel Kelly, in particular, has suffered from depression in the past and her book is separated into chapters according to problem e.g. lack of sleep, a need for balance, and a craving for comfort food. The introductions to each chapter make comforting reading if you need to know that you are not alone.

Action

❖ Plan your meals, down to lunches and snacks. It's easier to stay sensible when you know that there's a good meal ready and waiting to be cooked at home.

- ❖ If hunger strikes while you're out, have a drink of water. Very often we're actually thirsty when we feel hungry, and even if it is proper hunger the water will postpone the feeling until you get home or to a place where you can get something sensible to eat. I love sparkling water, since it makes me feel fuller quicker.

- ❖ If over-eating is your issue, keep an honesty diary as recommended by Lisa Riley in her book, Honesty Diet. She recommends writing down everything you eat, every drink, every sweet, every speck of food, noting when and what you were feeling at the time. It seems very nit-picky, but being honest and truthful with yourself about what you eat and why can have a big impact and encourage a healthier attitude to food.

Make Exercise A Part of Your Daily Life Rather Than a Bolt-On

I am a child of the 80's. When I was a teenager, Jane Fonda made it big with aerobics. Wearing legwarmers, going for the burn and being as stick thin as the models on her videos were common preoccupations amongst my fellow classmates. That was also the decade when VHS recorders and games consoles began to have an impact. Do you see the dichotomy here? As our leisure time became more sedentary, the idea of exercise as being something only done by the great and good took off.

I'm not an aerobics fan, but I do agree that exercise is vital for good health mentally and physically. I prefer to exercise in a way that suits me.

The best exercise will boost health and mood. Health benefits are boosted by exercise that raises the heart and respiration rate high enough to have a measurable effect. The maximum recommended heart rate for your age is easy enough to work out: take your age away from 220 and that should be the highest rate your heart beats during intensive exercise. So, for example, a 50-year old woman should exercise with a maximum heart rate of 170 beats per minute. How you do that, is up to you.

I like to integrate my exercise as much as possible. I love walking up and down my stairs a few more times than are strictly necessary, parking in the furthest spot from the store door, or not walking to the bus stop just outside my house but to one a few stops away so that I get a walk as part of the journey. Add a short walk after dinner most evenings or at lunchtime and enjoy the passing seasons as you pass the scenery. I love walking during the day, because I can get a blast of vitamin D as well, and a walk is a natural mood-booster.

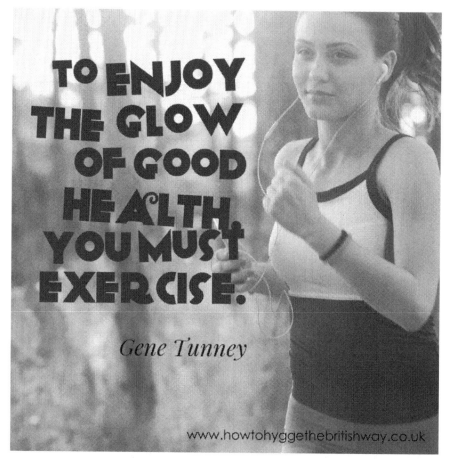

Experts recommend 10,000 steps a day as the optimal minimum, but if you can't get that done then any additional steps on top of your ordinary, everyday life have a benefit. You can also try walking or cycling instead of taking the car automatically, taking the stairs instead of any lifts and boosting exercise as much as possible.

Find exercise in unusual places as well: do squats at the oven, stretch over to reach for things and find ways to move your body as a part of everyday life. Cooking, cleaning and gardening are all good exercise if done with the right frame of mind. Stretch as much as you can, sit as little as possible and keep moving even when you sit down. Research shows people who fidget use more calories than those who keep still. It sounds silly, but it's true.

Action

- ❖ Make a list of possible ways to add more exercise into your life, no matter how silly they seem. Writing them down will make it more likely that you will incorporate them.
- ❖ Buy a pedometer or use the step counter on your phone to count your daily steps. Set yourself the challenge of doing more each day until you hit that 10,000 target.
- ❖ Need motivating? Find a walking buddy and set off for a chat as well as a wander, or download an app that aims to motivate you. Couch to 5k is a good one, and available free for most phones in the UK. Or, if you want fun as well as a run, try Zombies, Run! which combines a running app with a game. Outrun the zombies and collect supplies for the base! It is fun, and you can set it for walking or cycling as well.

Sleep Well

As a mother of newborns, I remember only too well the pain and mists that would come over me due to having a disturbed night. I had good babies and they slept well, usually right through from midnight to 6am from the age of two months. That six hours of undisturbed sleep was the best thing I could get most days. On the days when they were ill, or their routine had been disturbed (those crazy late afternoon drive homes when the baby fell asleep and woke up grumpy and hungry at 8 before refusing to go to sleep at the usual time) and they didn't sleep through, I got a short taste of what sleep deprivation felt like.

I had friends whose children didn't sleep through until they were three or four years old. I have no idea how they coped. The occasional day when I was hungry (hungry often goes with exhaustion for me), ready to shout at anybody who crossed me, living on coffee and chocolate to boost my sugar and caffeine content and crashing, exhausted, as soon as the husband walked in through the door was enough for me. That was before I knew how bad a lack of sleep could be for you as well.

Even a soul submerged in sleep is hard at work and helps make something of the world.

Heraclitus, Fragments

www.howtohyggethebritishway.com

Too little sleep impacts weight, heart, reaction times and pain threshold[7]. It's also bad for mood, sex life and immune system. Seriously, there is a reason that the CIA use sleep deprivation as a form of torture. It works.

So what can we do to boost sleep? Surprisingly, treating yourself as a baby works well. Set up a bedtime routine, keep to it and watch the sleep hours accumulate.

- Set a bedtime that suits you and keep to it as far as possible. Even if you are off work or out, your body will be happier if you stick to within an hour of your daily bedtime.

---

[7]   https://www.huffingtonpost.com/2015/01/28/biggest-sleep-health-bene_n_6549830.html

- Stop looking at anything electrical for at least an hour before bed. Turn off the TV, put down your smart phone, don't go for that last look on the computer. The blue light of electrical screens has been credited with disrupting our natural circadian rhythms.
- Have a warm bath or shower. Use a relaxing gel or oil such as lavender, rose, vanilla or sandalwood to help you relax.
- Drink a milky drink. Don't have anything caffeinated, but a warm milky drink can be such a relaxing thing. I love a last cup of tea, but I also love having a Horlicks or Ovaltine sometimes when I'm having the Ultimate Sleep Routine.
- Read something relaxing. You don't want to read an edge-of-the-seat thriller, but something soft and relaxing. I like reading one of my magazines sometimes, or a novel that I know won't keep me up. And set a limit of 10 to 20 minutes, after which you will put the book down and go to sleep.

That sounds so easy, but I know that sometimes you won't get to sleep straight away, or you'll wake up with a worry. Keep a notebook next to the bed to write any thoughts that creep into your head to disturb your sleep, write it down and lie back down.

And if you really aren't falling to sleep straight away? Get up, go into a different room and do something relaxing. I love to do a little easy crochet, or read for a while. I try not to watch Tv, because that pulls me wide awake. I make another warm drink, brush my teeth and settle back into bed.

Action

- ❖ Set out your routine. Decide what time bedtime is sensible for you and try to stick to it for a few days.
- ❖ Make a pact with yourself that you will not keep your phone on in the bedroom, even better if you promise not to keep it in the bedroom at all. The blue light from phones has been shown to be particularly detrimental.
- ❖ Find a drink that you can keep just for bedtime. I love a milky chai tea, with no sugar in, but a malted drink could be good.

Choose quality over quantity in all things

Our wardrobes are full of stuff. A 2016 survey for Oxfam found that 3.6 billion clothes lie unloved and unworn in British wardrobes[8] while another survey estimates that we wear 20% of our clothes 80% of the time, meaning that a large percentage of our wardrobe never sees the light of day.

What if we concentrated only on having that 20% we know we will wear? What if we wiped the slate clean and had only those things in our wardrobe that we know to be useful or believe make us look beautiful? (see William Morris comes in useful everywhere!) The other year I turned all the hangers in my wardrobe backwards, that is, instead of hooking them over the rail from the front I hooked them over from the back. Each time I wore something I replaced it hanging over from the front. By the end of the season I knew which Items I had reached for and worn, and which I had overlooked. I took the un-worn items out and put them to one side, and then looked at them carefully. Why wasn't I wearing them? Was it fit? Feel? Or just that they had been an impulse purchase and I had nothing that they actually went with?

Impulse buying is too easy to do. The modern fashion industry has grown to be incredibly wasteful of clothing. Fashions that change annually, or seasonally in some cases, and that use cheap resources abroad to manufacture and sell cheaply are built on obsolescence. They're designed not to last. It's too easy to pass by the rail in the shop or the supermarket and have our magpie eye captured by a colour or cut that we persuade ourselves we want. These purchases give our brain the buzz of buying without the pain of paying a lot for it. It's a very short-sighted view to take.

Inspired by a book called *The Happy Closet* by Annmarie O'Connor and Project 333, the minimalist fashion challenge created online by Courtney Carver, I looked at what I wore and when I wore it. I looked at the clothes I needed for work and home, the activities I seriously undertook and what I needed as a basic wardrobe for that and what a bare-bones wardrobe for me looked like, bearing in mind I am a bad housekeeper and need a good fortnight worth of clothes for washing purposes.

---

[8] https://www.oxfam.org.uk/media-centre/press-releases/2016/06/over-three-billion-clothes-left-unworn-in-the-nations-wardrobes-survey-finds

Buy less. Choose well. Make it last. Quality, not quantity. Everybody's buying far too many clothes.

Vivienne Westwood

www.howtohyggethebritishway.co.uk

Now I have a much better grasp of what clothes I like and use, what colours I love and what kinds of material suit me better. I focus not on shopping for quantity and having a wardrobe packed with bad choices, but on getting a good quality item that lasts, in colours that suit me and that go with a good percentage of my current clothes. I don't go shopping often, but when I do it's usually with a specific item in mind, like boots, or a coat. I am far from being able to keep to the 33 items for 3 months rule of Project 333, but I have cut the size of my wardrobe down, and keep doing so by regular clean outs and purges.

Action

❖ Go through your wardrobe twice a year, at the end of the summer and the end of winter. Sort out those items that have lost their sparkle, or that don't fit you any more.

❖ Make a list of items you really need, not just want and start browsing online and in shops for them. If you know you've looked and really can't find the item for such a good price anywhere else, a big buy will be easier to make.

❖ Start a 30-day waiting list for clothes. Before you buy anything new, you have to record it on a list and look out for it for 30 days. If you still need it after that length of time, then you can buy it (still after some sensible research)

Give a Girl the Right Shoes...

At some point in my early 30's I decided that anything remotely pretty shoe-like and heeled was not for me. I've worn sensible flat shoes for the past 20 years, and will probably be wearing them for the rest of my natural with no ill effects except if I wear ballerina pumps day-in, day-out, when my heels will start to hurt.

I'm in the minority there, though. Over 78% of British women wear high heels daily[9] despite them causing them pain after a mere one hour and six minutes. Not to mention the risks of back pain, ankle sprains, achilles tendon troubles and even a suggested increased risk of arthritis.... I just wouldn't be bothered.

My favoured footwear is boots. I just love wearing a solid pair of boots: ankle length or knee length, I love the fact that they cushion the sole, support the heel and more... much more than that... they make me feel like Wonder Woman.

My fascination goes back to my early years, as well, when a pair of red knee boots were my shoes of choice. My parents tell me I wore them all day every day, taking them off only to go to bed, and that I cried when the day came to part with them because, alas, my three-year-old feet had grown past them.

---

9   https://www.theguardian.com/lifeandstyle/2015/jun/21/are-high-heels-bad-for-your-feet

Give a girl the right shoes, and she can conquer the world.

Marilyn Monroe

I think I love boots because they give me that unbeatable feeling. In my boots, depending on what I wear with them, I can be either a pioneer woman striding around the plain and ready to shoot the bison I need for dinner, a space traveler on board the Enterprise and ready to discover the civilisations other spacemen left behind, or Wonder Woman herself: indomitable, invincible, but with a heart of purity and innocence. My boots, for me, are the shoes that free my spirit. They make me happy.

Action

- ❖ Find your perfect shoes. You may well be one of the few who can wear heels and feel like a super-confident business woman stomping the corridors of power. Or wear ballerinas in gentle colours or basic black and channel Audrey Hepburn, all grace and elegance in a small packet. I have a cousin who married in Doc Martens. She loved them, and she said they were her no-nonsense, cut the B-S boots for work (she was an engineer surrounded by men), so why not enjoy that feeling of power at her wedding as well?

- ❖ Take care of your shoes. Try to have two pairs which you alternate, if you can. Letting your shoes breathe will let them recover after a day out. Use socks or shoe liners to keep perspiration from entering the leather, clean regularly and use a small amount of bicarbonate of soda wrapped in the end of a laddered pair of tights to freshen them and soak up the smell between wears.

- ❖ Shoes, again, are a purchase where saving up and buying the best you can afford will make a difference to the quality. Looked after well, shoes can last quite a few years.

Scarves (and other accessories) are your best friend

When I limited my wardrobe and shed some of the multitude of tops I had purchased over the years, I worried that my clothes would look the same every day. I had forgotten the basic French Woman's advice: just stick a scarf on.

French women are renowned for their ability to tie a scarf in so many different ways that every day of the week it can look different. Books are available on Amazon telling you just how to tie the scarf in a multitude of ways, or Francophile blogs galore will tell you how to tie your scarf.

I love this article [10]from Huffington Post, which tells the story of how Susan Sisko Carter spent all the money in her purse one day on a beautiful scarf. The right scarf in the right

---

10   https://www.huffingtonpost.com/susan-sisko-carter/why-french-women-wear-sca_b_665490.html

colour can lift an outfit with a minimum of effort. I have a range of scarves in the colours that I know suit me: red, orange, a certain shade of blue and green. I usually use one when I'm wearing a black top which, for convenience, can't be bettered as an easy work uniform but has the habit of draining me of colour if I'm in the slightest feeling tired. Putting orange next to my face lifts my complexion and makes me feel happier every time I look in the mirror.

A splash of color will give you waves of enjoyment.

Anthony T.Hincks

www.howtohyggethebritishway.co.uk

I love accessories: I am rarely without a pair of earrings (usually made by my daughter: that makes them even more special to me) and an outfit isn't finished until I've chosen a bag that matches. I love colour, so I have bags in almost every shade I can afford. Bags, bought in the sales, can be cheap and always fit whatever size I'm feeling that day. Plus, again, with a sensible outfit at work, it can be good to add a pop of colour and individuality through my bag or scarf.

I don't ever go overboard, though. To have scarf, bag, earrings, necklace, bracelets, brooches and other accessories all on at once would really be overkill. I use Coco Chanel's philosophy: I look at myself before I go out and take one piece off. I want to look in a window as I go back and feel happy, not like a person weighed down just by accessories.

I do, however, play with my accessories sometimes. The right cloak can make me feel so much like a character in Poldark, or a flowing scarf makes me feel like an exotic 30s actress. For a few minutes I can be someone else, somewhere exotic, and doing something dangerous. Everybody needs a little playtime, don't we? Where a whole costume wouldn't look right, a small nod to our inner muse can give us a lift.

Action

- ❖ Don't be timid about accessories. Wear the scarf, put on the hat, choose the bag that makes you feel like a screen goddess. You deserve it, and if a bag or a bangle can make you feel happy, what's not to like?
- ❖ Take care of your accessories: hang scarves up, use a jewellery tree to display your collection, keep bags where you can see them and use them often.
- ❖ Accessories also act as memory catchers for me. I have a couple of scarves that I bought in Paris in 2011. I can tell you exactly which shop, and where I'd been that morning when I pick up the scarf. I have earrings from London that make me feel invincible, a bag that reminds me of a family wedding and well-loved but comfortable shoes that took me around York one cold, snowy weekend. If you're going to buy something on a trip, it may as well be useful.

A capsule wardrobe doesn't need to be black

I purged my wardrobe fully about three years ago. I purge it regularly, removing the clothes that I never wear, have outgrown, or that no longer fit my lifestyle. I keep reading about capsule wardrobes and there is a part of me that would love to be brave enough to cut my clothes down completely, but realistically I am a bad homemaker and my washing cycle can be anything between 24 hours and three weeks. I need enough clothes to see out a fortnight, reasonably, without washing.

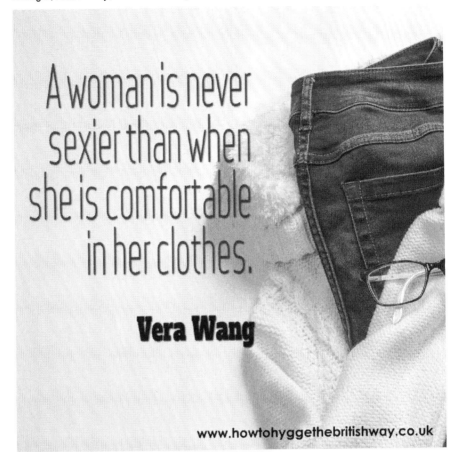

A woman is never sexier than when she is comfortable in her clothes.

Vera Wang

www.howtohyggethebritishway.co.uk

I also need my clothes to make me feel good. I want to be happy, so I need to know that when I pull on my jeans and a top, even if I do nothing more apart from tie my hair up and slick on a lip tint, I am fit to go out. I have no clothes that are too old or worn or battered to take me to the local shop. I learned that in my "Je Suis Parisienne" years.

There are hundreds of books on style and creating a workable wardrobe, each with a different approach. If you're after a good, basic guide to creating a workable capsule wardrobe, then The French Capsule Wardrobe by Renee Herrington is a simply written six-step guide with the underlying principle of a capsule wardrobe based on chic a la French girl to guide you. Or try The Happy Closet by Annmarie O'Connor (recommended earlier in the book as well).

The great thing I quickly found out about my capsule wardrobe was that, with me, it was never going to be just black, grey and beige. I look like death warmed up in grey and beige, and black is only wearable if I take great care to have colour next to my face. I have black basics, like my trousers or a couple of tops for work, but my tops are much more likely to be in a range of colours that suit me. I have red, orange, green and blue tops. They all go well together because I have kept to a range of colours that suit me according to the Colour Me Beautiful principle. For a basic guide to the principles and a push to align your wardrobe with the colour guidance, try Reinvent Yourself With Colour Me Beautiful by JoAnne Richmond.

I carried my capsule wardrobe colours through to my underwear as well. I love wearing matching underwear and believe that it helps to make a woman feel really sexy (regardless of whether she has anybody to feel sexy for) even if the only place she's going to is the playground with her children. I have green underwear, red undies, cream, blue and a few sets of passionate purple that I wear everyday, with a big smile on my face and knowing that if the worst every happens, my underwear will stand up to being scrutinized by a doctor in A & E. Colour makes me happy. It just does.

Action

- ❖ Use the advice on the internet or book a consultation (which can be quite pricey) to have your colours done. It is amazing how wearing the shades that match you lift your complexion and make you feel better. Print out and laminate the shade card for your colours, and carry it with you when you go shopping at first. After a while, you will know what colours you feel best in.
- ❖ Start curating your wardrobe. Consider which clothes you need for which events, and start rationalizing your clothes according to requirement and lovability. You need to really love your clothes to justify them taking up the space in your closet.
- ❖ Have a list of the very minimum you need in your wardrobe. Some books recommend a limit of 30 pieces of clothing, but that seems harsh to me. If you've worked out what lifestyle events you have, you can start from there and list what clothes you have that would suit each event. Make sure you have tops and jackets that coordinate: that's easier than it used to be, when fashion rules were stricter and you could never get away with red and green, or blue and orange.

Wear the colours you love and that love you, you can always link two different colours by using a scarf or accessories that have both the colours in.

A Little of What You Fancy Does You Good

There is nothing worse than sitting on a diet and never but never eating anything that gives your soul a lift. If you are trying hard to lose weight then it seems harsh but you can't have cakes, biscuits, processed food, fast food or whatever your personal eating trigger may be every day.

Neither can you do without forever without risking a complete melt-down and a binge on the stupidest things. One day I was so desperate for a proper custard tart that I took the car and drove to the nearest supermarket that did them, I was after a proper one, not just mass-produced ones but thick, dusted with nutmeg and with a layer of sweet pastry thick enough to be pick-up-able without being mouth-cloggingly bad for me.

The supermarket had none in. They were sold out.

Now, fortunately for me that was the wake-up call I needed that day to make sure that I walked out of the shop and went home. I ate my green apple, sliced and served on a plate with glass of sparkling water.

Hygge and Lagom are all about balance. You can't have the cakes and sweets every day unless you balance them with healthy eating and healthy living as well. I like being sensible. The diet I am currently on and losing weight on is a variation of the 5:2 diet called The Dirty Diet. It's based on the principle of fasting for two days a week and eating sensibly for the rest of the week, but on those five days you can eat whatever you like. The fasting days are carefully controlled, 500 to 700 calories a day, but the ordinary days are more relaxed. It's been a godsend for me, because I can actually plan my days of deprivation and plenty. And because you are only ever really strict for 24 hours total, you can keep focused and good on that day, knowing that whatever craving you want you can freely have the next day. It's surprising how often you find you don't want the item the next day.

If you're desperate to have that treat, but really want to keep it healthy, then there are some ways to cheat a little.

Tom Kerridge's *Lose Weight for Good* contains favourite recipes that have been taken and tweaked so that they contain less calories and still have flavour. It has a chapter on baking and treats but warns that you should have them, not everyday, but just occasionally, as a treat.

Red Velvet and Chocolate Heartache by Harry Eastwood takes your favourite deliciously decadent desserts and uses vegetables instead of sweetening or fat in some recipes to make cakes that fool your eye and your taste bud.

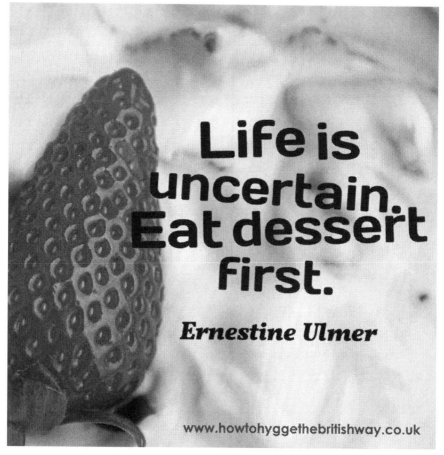

Remember, though, this is not you breaking your diet and going mad with the calories afterwards, this is an occasional treat. If you're going to do it, do it well.

Make a ceremony of it: set a tray with a cloth, flower bud in a vase, milk jug, cup and saucer and a plate with a select portion of your treat on it. Make a pot of tea or coffee, go into your living room, light a candle, put on the fairy lights and sit back to have a proper teatime treat.

I love enjoying afternoon tea at home with my children, and have done since they were small. Even a packet of jelly tots seems like a big treat if you make enough fuss of it. You're worth it, and life is made to be celebrated.

Action:

* ❖ Enjoy a little of what you fancy. Make sure that you really want the treat you're planning: make a ceremony of it, with a pot of tea or coffee, plate, knife and fork. Never mindlessly eat something. That's asking for trouble!

* ❖ On a diet? Desperate to indulge? Most diets are sensible enough to allow the occasional treat. Look up the advice for your diet, or fall back on the classic stand by of fruit and chocolate. Choose some seasonal fruit, strawberries are particularly good, and slice them up. Arrange them on a plate. Melt a couple of squares of chocolate in a small bowl. Dip the fruit and enjoy free from guilt.

* ❖ Balance any treats you have with some exertion. Walk, play football, clean the house or garden, any physical activity that uses up energy and makes you sweat will help balance your life.

Happiness In Your Own Body Resources

Websites and Articles

http://blogs.plos.org/obesitypanacea/2010/10/18/10-simple-ways-to-increase-your-physical-activity/ An easy list of 10 everyday things to do to boost your exercise levels.

https://www.huffingtonpost.com/2015/01/28/biggest-sleep-health-bene_n_6549830.html The benefits of getting enough sleep.

https://www.nosleeplessnights.com/sleep-hygiene/bedtime-routine-for-adults/ Establishing a bedtime routine for an adult. This article also contains advice on what to do when you don't fall off to sleep straight away!

https://bemorewithless.com/project-333/ All the information you need, and a lot of advice, on starting your own minimalist clothes experiment.

https://www.theguardian.com/lifeandstyle/2015/jun/21/are-high-heels-bad-for-your-feet Why not to wear heels, and advice for if you must.

http://www.thespinehealthinstitute.com/news-room/health-blog/how-high-heels-affect-your-body How do high heels affect the body if worn too often?

https://www.realsimple.com/beauty-fashion/shoes-accessories/shoes/care-for-shoes Caring for your shoes to help them last as long as possible is not only sensible: it can save you cash in the longrun.

https://www.vagabomb.com/13-Quotes-from-French-Fashion-Icons-through-the-Ages-Which-Define-French-Style/ Irresistible quotes about French style, and how they find their own way to be... well, so very French!

https://www.huffingtonpost.com/susan-sisko-carter/why-french-women-wear-sca_b_665490.html This is a beautiful story of why sometimes it's worth spending every penny on just that one perfect item... le couleur d'une bonne nuit.

Books

The Happy Kitchen by Rachel Kelly

Lose Weight For Good by Tom Kerridge

The Honesty Diet by Lisa Riley

The Happy Closet by Annmarie O'Connor

The French Capsule Wardrobe: French Secrets to Style, Minimalism and Simple Elegance by Renee Herrington

Reinvent Yourself With Colour Me Beautiful by JoAnne Richmond

The Dirty Diet: Ditch the Guilt and Love Your Food by Kate Harrison. A good, working version of the 5:2 diet, with good recipes and explanations of how the diet works.

Lose Weight For Good: Full-flavour cooking for a Low-Calorie Diet by Tom Kerridge.Tom takes common family favourites and cooks them in a healthier way. The book includes bakes and desserts.

Red Velvet and Chocolate Heartache by Harry Eastwood. Cakes made with vegetables or fruit to make them a little more healthy.... Not guilt-free but guilt-lite

Keeping Your Mind Happy:

When the body is healthy, the chances of keeping the mind healthy increase tremendously. As the latin phrase goes, *Mens sana in corpore sano* (A healthy mind in a healthy body). The last chapter had ideas for improving your physical life: this chapter is about letting your mind play for itself. It's about using the world around you to build resilience towards the knocks of life, feeding your mind with the information it needs to build a strong support network and about encouraging your mind to grow through study and play.

This chapter is concerned with the thinking part of your brain, as I have separated out our spirits into the intellectual, rational part and the emotional, soul-full part. It should give you some ideas for ways to stretch yourself, even if your job doesn't, and ways to keep your brain working in a positive way rather than letting it brood on things that might dampen your mood.

Biology gives you a brain. Life turns it into a mind.

Jeffrey Eugenides

www.howtohyggethebritishway.co.uk

We Read to Know We're Not Alone

One thing that comes up again and again in my life is the value that reading has in helping me feel that I am not alone in my problems, or alternatively that there is always someone else worse off than me. I have never knowingly been without a book in my hands or my bag, either a physical book or an ebook on my Kindle. I was 13 and hating secondary school when I first discovered how useful books could be in restoring my equilibrium. When the Deputy Headteacher chose to take against me for reasons only she knows, I found books gave me emotional support better than any human at school and entry into a host of worlds that I preferred to stay in.

Our minds are shaped by the books we read.

Robin S. Sharma

www.howtohyggethebritishway.co.uk

I escaped, absolutely and utterly, into a different world. I don't think I have ever had so much time to read (when you don't have much homework, there's nothing on TV and you don't go out much, there's a lot of time to fill and books fill that time well) as my early teenage years. I loved historical romance (Georgette Heyer got me through my O level

History), science fiction that took me to the outer reaches of the galaxy and read a load of Classics, those big, thick doorstops of books that were available cheaply in paperback version simply on the spurious excuse that their authors died in Victorian or Edwardian times.

I learned much from all my reading: I built a picture of Victorian England that I wanted simultaneously to live in and never visit. I acquired a distrust of authoritarianism and dictated thought that has stayed with me. It shaped me as a human being, made me think about what I wanted out of life and even, in several cases, gave me inspiration for how I wanted my house to be when I got one (see *The Harvester* by Gene Stratton Porter for a beautifully hygge house)

I still love reading, although I can't read at the same speed and volume as I used to. I still read historical novels and classics, although my science fiction reading has tipped more to the fantasy. I also read more and more self-help books, often looking for advice or inspiration from people in the same or similar situation to me. Good books stay with me, bad books get given away.

Never be afraid to reread a favourite book. I have a bookshelf in my bedroom that is filled with the books that I would call my keepers... the ones that would be the first things I unpacked at a new house and the last books I'd give away (*Simple Abundance*, *Jane Eyre* and *The Harvester*, to name a few). And I have something similar with my Kindle: a collection of the books that I love having with me wherever I am, since the ability to dip into them for comfort and inspiration at any time is a real treasure. In the case of my favourite books, I don't need to read the whole book again, just to reread the sections that are most meaningful to me.

As I age, I find that self-help and factual books take up a lot more of my time. They encourage me to think through what I want, how I want to be and what steps I need to take to make my life better. I will often read two or three books around the same time about the same particular area, for example, curating a capsule wardrobe, and then choose the best bits from each to apply. I've been doing that with books about boosting creativity this year, reading *Big Magic* by Elizabeth Gilbert as well as *Year of Yes* by Shonda Rhimes and *Art & Soul Reloaded* by Pam Grout. I glean the best ideas from all of them to help create my own life.

Action

❖ Join Goodreads to keep a record of what you have read and when. Each book entry comes with reviews by the community, lists that the book is on, and other books by the same author. You can also enter a key word and receive recommendations.

❖ Join a local book club to stretch your reading. A good book club will often push you to read a book that you wouldn't have voluntarily chosen. Look in the local library, bookshop, or very often a café will have a community board. Don't see one? Start one! I couldn't find a club that suited me, so I set it up.

❖ Keep a book diary. It's interesting to keep a list of the books that you have read, with a couple of lines on what you thought or felt about the book, and then to read through a few years later and see how the books you like or the responses to those books may have changed.

❖ Bibliotherapy is the use of books to help heal mental illnesses. The right book at the right time can help one to bridge the dark places in life. *The Novel Cure* by Ella Berthould and Susan Elderkin look at a wide range of illnesses and emotions through the lens of books that may help. It's very much in the "We read to know we're not alone" idea. I love the description of it as a 'literary tonic'.

Using films as medication

In a similar way, using films as medication can work as well. Bernie Wooder explained in an interview in the Telegraph[11], "Films provide role models, clarify relationship issues, identify problems and solutions, inspire and motivate. And because you watch from a third person perspective, your defences are down, so the film can act as a springboard for self-discovery."

Films have the advantage over novels in being full colour (usually) and providing an immersive experience. With the right combination of story, characters, music and meaning

---

11   http://www.telegraph.co.uk/news/health/3330249/Movie-therapy-Do-you-believe-in-the-healing-power-of-film.html

a film can reach out and touch you. I'm a sucker for films, especially if they use music well. Don't laugh, but the first few minutes of Star Trek (2009) has me in tears every time, and sets me up to be sympathetic to a rather annoyingly badly behaved James Kirk. Seeing him win through against a rough start is a prime example of the mythical hero making good. Cinematherapy.com[12] says that "Many films contain a mythical message that reminds us of our virtue and our authentic self." And, indeed, with their shorter time frame and often a requirement to have a simpler plot, a film can reach the mythical impact in two hours that a novel takes a week over. Both have a place in restoring our balance and creating happiness.

Which films to watch? Well, a quick search for 'inspirational films' will give you a long list, or pop over to which ever social media you like best and ask there. A quick question on The

---

[12] http://www.cinematherapy.com/whyitworks.html

Hygge Nook garnered over 100 responses within a day, and a wide range of films from The Shawshank Redemption to Meet Joe Black. There were too many to list here, but I have a post on my blog about using favourite films for Cinema Therapy, if you go through to www.howtohyggethebritishway.com and search for cinema therapy. Otherwise, keep watching the movies you love and noticing what effect they have on you personally. Sometimes a film that makes you happy can be the cinematic equivalent of a peeled onion to a friend, while the laughter-guaranteed road movie that had your partner rolling in the aisles leaves you feeling bereft and unloved. We bring our own selves to both books and films, and what the message of the movie is depends on your life and experiences.

I keep a list in my notebook ready to turn to when things are bad and I need to watch something. Separating the list into good laughs, weepies and inspirational films helps.

Action:

- ❖ Listen to film reviews to find the next film on your list. I love Kermode and Mayo's Film Review[13] on BBC Radio 5. I find I usually agree with their conclusions, and the interaction between the two of them is funny. Plus also I love their self-named "Church of Wittertainment[14]", with the Cinema Code of Conduct including such obvious things as no rustling, no phone usage and no removing shoes.

- ❖ Make that page in your planner! Divide it into Weepies, Inspirational and Feel Good movies and then get listing.

- ❖ Have an emergency film kit ready for the day you need it: popcorn or chocolate and a cup of tea can make a difference when comfort is all you need.

- ❖ There is great power in going to the cinema alone. If a film resonates with you and nobody else wants to see it, then why not take yourself off on a creative excursion. The best advantage is that in the dark of the cinema, no one can see you cry.

---

[13] http://www.bbc.co.uk/programmes/b00lvdrj

[14] http://witterpedia.net/wiki/index.php?title=Church_of_Wittertainment

---

Ration your time on social media effectively

Whether you love it or loathe it, social media is here to stay. From Facebook to Twitter to Instagram and Whatsapp, there's a platform to share your views and news on. As a blogger, politics nerd and crafter I find the whole social media thing absolutely necessary to build an audience and link with people who like the things I do. That's both the positive and the negative side of social media, since building virtual bridges between people possibly means that the physical links between real people don't get the attention they deserve.

I also enjoy meeting opposing views on social media. We are in danger of becoming too tribal in the 21st Century, apt to believe that because everybody on our Twitter feed agrees with us, that view point is the same the country or world over. It's not, of course. We edit our feeds, often to find people who think as we do. Perhaps the safety of online living is the fact that a discussion always stays verbal. We may argue the toss with a person at the other end of the country, but we know if things get too much we can always block or mute them. The only person I have been blocked by, as far as I know, is a crafter after an argument that turned political. It's a shame, as I enjoyed experiencing a completely different way of living. I never minded if her political views were different than mine: tolerance is what makes us humans rather than animals. I do not block or mute for opposing views. Life is too short, and a good friendship can survive a verbal argument or two. I will block if the arguments get personal, or begin to affect my everyday life. As long as I leave Twitter behind when I turn off the phone, I am okay.

There are times on social media when things get really bitter. Elections, times of attack, when something really divisive is on TV. Go on a feed then and you can see the splits that can be caused. In the UK in 2016, the Brexit referendum really had people at each other's throats. You were one side or the other, and the vitriol posted by both sides was bitter, angry.... Really vindictive. People are always going to be separated by belief in politics, religion or even whether Eastenders is better than Coronation Street but whichever argument it is, surely respect for everyone else as people should mean a sensible argument is possible? Actually, that's a pipe dream. There will always be people who see social media as a chance to be rude, to post their inner demons to whoever is the centre of their hatred that day. It becomes necessary then to find a way to engage without losing faith in the good of humanity.

SOCIAL MEDIA IS THE ULTIMATE EQUALIZER. IT GIVES A VOICE AND A PLATFORM TO ANYONE WILLING TO ENGAGE.

Amy Jo Martin

www.howtohyggethebritishway.co.uk

I use a four-step plan to keep my social media pleasant enough to look at:

1. Have different social media for different parts of your life. I use Facebook for personal life, and for How to Hygge the British Way. Instagram is eye candy, mostly hygge or guinea pig based. Twitter is my dark side, my political or protest side. I know when I've been on Twitter too long because I grow cynical and bitter. My Twitter feed is like the portrait in the attic: a side I have but don't always want to look at. I use Twitter a lot when there's something big in the news and I want to interact.

2. Leave your charger in an out of the way place. I have my charger upstairs, so that when I get home and want to charge the battery I have to take the phone upstairs and leave it there. That forces me to interact with the humans around me.

3. Be careful who you link up to, and don't be afraid to defriend or unfollow. You have a right to a positive feed, so if anybody is making you feel uncomfortable or

bringing out the inner witch in you, just lose them from your life.

4.   Create your own content, so there's always something positive to look at. When life gets you down, post a good quote. Feeling blue? Share a puppy picture.

Making quotes is easy, and sharing content will make other people's days as well. Time spent on the computer needs looking at as well. Now that I work all day long on a computer, I am less likely to want to spend an evening trawling through sites and browsing, but I know the lure of online shopping, watching programmes and social media. The whimsically named nomophobia[15], the fear of missing out on virtual connection, is now a real issue, with many spending more time connected to each other by their computer or phone than joining up in real life. Leave the computer, drop the phone, ring up your friend and get out to enjoy real people. Be sensible and enjoy the wonders of technology responsibly.

Action

❖   Make yourself put down the phone. You and your family are entitled to be unavailable for hours at a time. Once you leave the office, you owe nothing to nobody.

❖   Worried about the children? Read around and get as much advice as you can, talk to the children and be realistic. You won't ever eliminate screen time completely, but you can hopefully achieve a balance.

❖   Make the alternative to screen time appealing. That might be a bottle of cider and a film some nights, but it could be going out for a coffee, having a walk or flying a kite on another day.

❖   Remember you don't know what the person on the other end is going through. That crafter that blocked me? She had depression and found my Northern blunt common sense too much to handle. I won't chase her, I won't bother her again. I just wish her well in the future and hope she finds a pathway through her blackness.

---

[15] The name comes from no-mobile-phobia

Learn a language

Jeg laerer dansk[16]. Not a lot, but I'm trying. As part of my love for hygge, I also have a great respect for Denmark and the other Scandinavian and Nordic countries. I think it was The Killing that first made me want to speak the language. Apparently, it is the hardest European language to learn. I set out to be able to listen to both The Killing and Borgen without subtitles. I'm still working on it, but that's my own fault.

Fluent in 3 Months by Benny Lewis is a really good book full of advice on how to learn a language in three months. Benny speaks seven languages confidently and can converse in many more. His book is full of advice, links and ideas to make learning language easier. His advice is to be a language hacker, and not to worry about making mistakes. He even offers a week-long email course via his website and his TED talks on language hacking are really good and available on Youtube[17]

Learning a language needn't cost a lot: The app, Duolingo is free and doesn't limit the number of languages you want to learn while Babbel also does good deals on 3 or 6 month packages, enabling you to learn as quickly or as slowly as you want. Old textbooks are available on Amazon, often for very little, and it is usually possible to find a speaker of most languages living nearby who may be happy to meet up for coffee and talk to you. Facebook is useful for this. If you choose a more common language such as Spanish or French you will find more people to talk to.

I speak languages indifferently, mostly because I'm slightly deaf and I struggle to hear different sounds in the languages but I read and translate a lot of languages to some degree or another, a useful skill on holidays when I enjoy working out what I think things say before finding out if I'm right. I learned French at secondary school, and some of that must have stuck with me although I always thought of myself as a bad speaker. Knowledge of one language leads to others. Knowing some French made Italian and Spanish easier to understand, in a way. I find Danish has a lot of words in common with English, or German. I'm building the links between language families as I go along.

---

[16] I am learning Danish

[17] https://www.youtube.com/results?search_query=benny+lewis

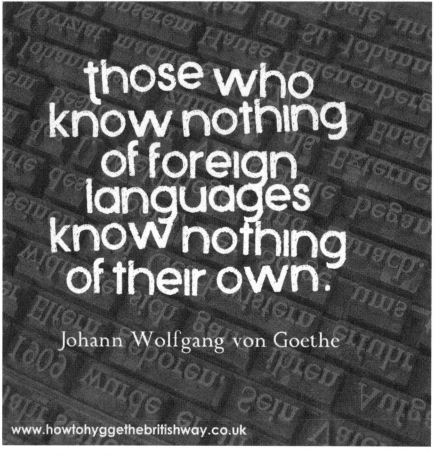

those who
know nothing
of foreign
languages
know nothing
of their own.

Johann Wolfgang von Goethe

www.howtohyggethebritishway.co.uk

I can read French well enough that I no longer translate it in my head. I never actually thought that was possible: how on earth does anyone actually think in another language? Benny Lewis says that the only way to learn a language is to talk it, to ignore any excuses your brain thinks of and speak it to whoever you meet. Be prepared to make mistakes, to make people laugh and to spend some time apologizing for your proficiency. But talk.

Actually, I learned how to handle French well enough by saturating myself with it. By reading anything in French that I could find, by watching French movies, by subscribing to a women's magazine in French. It's amazing how much vocabulary you pick up in a magazine that basically shadows the magazines you read most often in your own language.

Action:

- ❖ Feel inspired? Choose a language and start today.
- ❖ Download Duolingo. It offers a host of languages to learn for free.
- ❖ Join a Facebook learning group for that language and try to find someone near to you who is happy to come and talk with you over coffee and cake.
- ❖ The internet is great for finding things to read. You can find magazines, books or blogs in every language. Blogs are really good, because again you can find ones that suit you. Some bloggers write in both their own language and English, so you can read the original and then check against the writer's translation.

Study a culture other than your own

When we were first going out and married (pre-children) the Husband and I loved travelling. Going places on holiday, visiting Europe, City breaks. We travelled as hard as we could afford to, in anticipation of a few year's break when we wouldn't make it to another country or, if we did, we would be accompanied by a little person who made long, slow afternoons people watching at a pavement café difficult.

How wise we were. We didn't have either the spare cash or the will to go abroad for a while after the children came. We first left all of them for a European weekend break to celebrate 10 years together, so our youngest (of three) was then only 18 months old. We were lucky that my parents were healthy, fit and willing to take on three children from 18 months to 5 and a half for a weekend.

We went to Paris and, although it wasn't my first time there, it was my first proper escape from motherhood and I fell in love with what I saw as an alternative lifestyle. I think we both might have sat at a pavement café one afternoon and muttered (shame-facedly) "If we hadn't had children, we'd have done this a lot more." I would never have given up my children for that alternate universe, but it was fun to play that part for a weekend.

When I returned, I decided that enough was enough. There was nothing stopping me enjoying a cosmopolitan French lifestyle at home, it was just a matter of make-believe. I invested time and effort in becoming a Parisienne. I read whatever books I could find, watched as many films and programmes as I could find and tried to live in a very stereotypical Parisienne fashion, with matching underwear, chic coordinated outfits and a belief that I was beautiful just as I was.

WHEREVER YOU GO BECOMES A PART OF YOU SOMEHOW.

Anita Desai

www.howtohyggethebritishway.co.uk

In the past 15 years I have lived Parisienne, flirted with Italian and love Danish. I have read the books about the lifestyles, borrowed or bought recipe books and learned to cook in the style of, watched TV and films either set in the countries or made by the people from the countries. Living Danish led me to hygge, which has led me to feeling content with where I am now. My next Country to explore may well be the United Kingdom, as I seek out the hidden gems in this country. Or I might go Hawaiian, Jamaican or Japanese. It depends which culture catches my attention next. I think this summer will be a return to Italy, and my honeymoon since we celebrate 25 years together.

I love to read up on the history and the culture of my adopted alter-ego. I like knowing what shapes a country, how old or new it is, and what influences it has. Finding exhibitions of artwork, or looking up the great works of art online, is useful. It's interesting to see what elements of the art get absorbed by other cultures.

And I like to plan my fantasy trip to my cultural obsession. I may never get to go on it, but the fun is as much in the planning as the execution.

Action:

❖ Why not be an armchair traveler? Choose a country that has fascinated you and invest some time in make believe. What is the culture like? The food? The government system? Indulge in some recipe books and introduce the traditional food of your chosen country to your repertoire.

❖ Some countries are easier than others, simply because a lot of people have always aspired to be or to study their ways. France is a fine example. You can find visitors writing about France going back to the 18th Century and earlier. In my Francophile years I found several books really useful. I have listed these in the resources section. Likewise, Italy and Denmark both turned up trumps with loads of resources.

Be a Lifelong Learner to expand your horizons

There is nothing like being a supply teacher for testing your resourcefulness. Turning up at a school where you have been promised 'full plans and worksheets will be ready for you' to find out that the plans are still in the (absent) teacher's bag and the worksheets never made it to the photocopier is a good test of your ability to think on your feet. Especially when it turns out that the science lesson planned is an area you know little about and has to be done in sequence because... well, there's always a reason.

Learning about new stuff and new skills has never stopped fascinating me. I love weird and wonderful documentaries, about engineering, space, history (I love history a lot!) and basically anything that catches my attention. And living in the information age, there are so many sources of information and learning that you will never be lost for something to do.

First source, of course, is books. Whether your learning is official, like continuous professional development for work or a step towards a qualification, or you just want to learn about something for the sake of it, there will be a book published about it already. Non-fiction books are compelling. I find they give you information, widen experience and can influence your life. I divide them in my life into text books and self-help books.

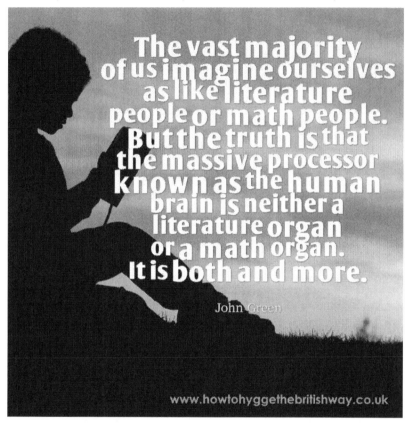

The vast majority of us imagine ourselves as like literature people or math people. But the truth is that the massive processor known as the human brain is neither a literature organ or a math organ. It is both and more.

John Green

www.howtohyggethebritishway.co.uk

Text books are the factual tomes that tell you about a subject. They're often analytical, focused on the transfer of facts and very often big, thick volumes that take up a lot of space. They also usually take too long to read to make borrowing them from a library a good idea unless you are that organised person who remembers to renew the due date by telephone or over the internet. I have borrowed them, only to be hit by the maximum fines by the time I returned them. My husband is a history buff, so a big book makes a fine birthday or Christmas present for him. Top history books I've read are Antonia Fraser's *Marie Antoinette* and Tracey Borman's *Thomas Cromwell*. I have these both on audio books as well, because sometimes I enjoy listening to a good, solid non-fiction book when I'm cleaning or travelling. You can learn a lot with a paintbrush in hand.

I know self-help books can be over-rated, and some hit the big time simply because they have been over-hyped, but a good self-help book will always have a take-home point, something useful for the life ahead. I love reading the best of them. I like to have them in book form, not Kindle, and go through, pencil in hand, marking off lines and passages that speak to me. I'm on a budget, so very often I buy them secondhand, if I'm not getting them for a present, and sometimes you meet other people's thoughts in them. Whatever your issue, there will be a guide out there for you. Ask on Twitter and Facebook for ideas, and read the books pages of magazines like *Project Calm* or *In The Moment* to find the next good thing. I've listed quite a few in this book, simply because I love a good book that sends you off in search of more goodness. If they've been useful or good to me, why not pass the recommendation on?

My current read is *Happy* by Fearne Cotton. Its subtitle is *Finding Joy in Every Day and Letting Go Of Perfect*. I'm enjoying it very much: it has great ideas for thoughts and actions to keep you balanced, and increase the chances of staying within your happy area. Small actions make a difference, that's the secret of being happier.

I also love to watch and learn. Seeking out a good documentary and watching it can be a valuable source of learning. Without leaving our own homes, we can travel through time with one presenter, voyage to the stars with another and delve into the depths of the human psyche with a third. Look out on the hidden channels for subjects that interest you, or make a promise to watch one not-so-interesting documentary a week and see what new things you can learn. Sometimes, our best educations come from areas we know nothing about and, thus, come to with no expectations.

Ditto with Ted talks and other online documentary video series. It should be easy to find one in your interest area, but remember to stretch your viewing occasionally by watching stuff outside of your comfort zone. Stepping outside of your comfort zone is something we should do in all walks of life, as long as there's no risk involved. With Ted talks, the time outlay often results in new knowledge and a wider view of the world than when you started. You will hear people who, in real life, you'd never get near. One of my favourite Ted Talk lists is the one on The Importance of Self Care, with people like Brene Brown, Andy

Puddicombe and Carl Honore all talking about the value of balance[18].

If you struggle to keep paying attention unless you're involved and doing something, you may find online courses in different things more useful. There's a wide choice of subjects, either academic or personal development, and a wide range of costs. Some courses are self-guided, others have a weekly structure and lead to qualifications. Choosing a course that adds to your employability or choosing to study one just for fun, whichever reason you have to study, being open to new learning and new experiences keeps your brain active and enhances life. Future Learn offers free online courses in a wide variety of subjects. Go, and see what you fancy.

I've barely touched the surface of life-long learning here. Finding and attending free lectures, concerts, theatre trips on days when the cast come out afterwards, reading any and everything put in front of you, asking the questions and finding the answers, going to quizzes, being on quiz shows. Every day is a new learning experience. Go: and make the most of them.

Action:

- ❖ Sign up for notifications from your local museums or art galleries so that you get advanced notice of any lectures or mini-workshops they may have.
- ❖ Choose an area and play-learn in it. Dipping your toe in and reading around the subject, taking a free online course or attending a couple of lectures will give you a grounding that you can expand on.
- ❖ Not into anything academic? Then go practical, with horticulture, crafts or art as your focus. The same rules apply.

---

[18] https://www.ted.com/playlists/299/the_importance_of_self_care

Keeping Your Mind Happy Resources

Websites and Articles

https://www.goodreads.com/ The Book Site for sharing what you are reading now, what you want to read and what you thought about what you read. It's easy to put books on your virtual shelf, set up groups, find and follow friends and use Goodreads for a variety of things. My daughter loves entering competitions to try and win books.

https://www.telegraph.co.uk/news/health/3330249/Movie-therapy-Do-you-believe-in-the-healing-power-of-film.html The healing power of film. It's what the film leaves you with that counts.

http://www.cinematherapy.com/whyitworks.html The mythic qualities of films can help us see issues in our own lives more clearly.

https://www.bbc.co.uk/programmes/b00lvdrj Kermode and Mayo's Film Review home page on the BBC. A podcast worth finding and listening to if you love films.

https://www.instagram.com/britishhyggejem/ My Instagram. I use this for hygge and happiness, little snippets of personal life and sharing the quotes from my blog and books.

https://www.facebook.com/howtohyggethebritishway/ Every serious blogger has a Facebook page to share posts on. I share other stuff here as well, but for proper hygge sharing I prefer:

https://www.facebook.com/groups/TheHyggeNook/ where hygge from across the World is shared by the members. We have people from all walks for life, and sharing their moments of happiness makes others happier as well.

https://www.duolingo.com/ A free app available on computer or phone that will encourage you to learn a language through reading, listening and talking it.

https://uk.babbel.com/ is a subscription-based service similar to Duolingo.

http://www.calmmoment.com/ is the website for Project Calm and In The Moment, magazines that both offer mindfulness and stress relief through creativity and crafting.

https://www.ted.com/playlists/299/the_importance_of_self_care A full Ted playlist to watch all at once or broken into parts. With experts like Brene Brown, Andy Puddicombe and Carl Honore, it's a programme you'd never afford to attend in real life.

https://www.futurelearn.com/ is a website full of free online courses run by some of the best universities in the world. They may run only at certain times, so keep an eye out and sign up when you see them.

Books

The Harvester by Gene Stratton Porter. I love the house, hand-made by the hero, and the description of the interiors.

Jane Eyre by Charlotte Bronte. Sometimes the most powerful books of your life are those you meet in early adulthood. I was 13 when I first read this.

Big Magic by Elizabeth Gilbert. When opportunity knocks, you don't have to say yes unless you want to… but if you do, you want Big Magic on your side. A look at creativity and how it can work for you.

Year of Yes by Shonda Rhimes. Even the most successful women feel the fear: Shonda's book shows how she stopped saying no and said yes instead… and how that made her life even better.

Art and Soul Reloaded by Pam Grout. I think I've recommended this elsewhere as well. A good book is a good book. With chapters set out to follow weekly, the book helps guide you to a more creative life.

The Novel Cure: An A to Z of Literary Remedies by Ella Berthoud and Susan Elderkin. Depressed? There's a book for that. In love? Yes, one for that too. Read at the right time, a book can change your life and the writers have gathered a medical handbook with a difference.

Fluent in 3 Months by Benny Lewis. Think you can't learn a foreign language? So did Benny, and then he decided enough was enough and he'd just go for it.

The Killing TV Series In the original Danish. This was the thing that got me into hygge. Yes, it's the most uhygge story, but look at the interiors, look at the jumper….

Borgen TV Series. More Danishness. I love seeing a woman who looks like a real woman, rather than a model-perfect actress, as the PM.

Living French: The books I found useful in making my home more chic or charming.

Bonjour Happiness by Jamie Cat Callan. Jamie has a few books out, all mostly based on the theme of finding your real self by looking at how French women act. I found them useful for boosting my self-confidence, and enjoyable reads.

Forever Chic: French Women's Secrets for Aging With Style and Grace by Tish Jett. French women do know how to age well... perhaps because they are allowed to? It's not about the numbers, it's about style, simplicity, intelligence and generosity.

Inspired by Paris: Why Borrowing from the French is Better Than Actually Being French by Jordan Phillips. Because sometimes you don't really want to visit a place to get a taste of it. It's a good book for getting a lightening tour of the people and places that make Paris the centre of everything that it is.

Lessons From Madame Chic by Jennifer L Scott. Based on her year living with a French family, Jennifer shows how the basics of charming French living can be transfered across the sea (in her case, to America). Jennifer has two further Parisienne charm books, focusing on making everyday life a more pleasant and elegant experience wherever you are in the world. I love them all.

Seeking Hygge? In my search for why Danes were happy, I read anything. These are my top picks.

The Cozy Life: Rediscover the Joy of Simple things through the Danish Concept of Hygge by Pia Edberg. Small changes make a big difference to life in the end. The book shows you how making a cozy life makes you happier.

The Nordic Guide to Living 10 Years Longer by Bertil Marklund. Living NOrdically means more than hygge. It's about balance and being healthy in mind and body as well.

North: How to Live Scandinavian by Bronte Aurell. Bronte owns and runs The Scandinavian Kitchen in London, and the shop website often features ideas to #livemorenordic

How to Hygge by Signe Johansen gives hints for living a more Norwegian life, full of fresh air and exercise.

Turning Italian? Look for La Dolce Vita in these books.

Living La Dolce Vita by Raeleen D'Agostino Mautner. Community and togetherness make Italian living a good source for happiness seekers. The book makes a good case for looking at the Italian lifestyle to boost your own.

La Bella Figura: How to Live a Chic, Simple and European-Inspired Life by Kristi Belle. Along with her other book, *La Dolce Vita: Living the Sweet Life for Less*, it's like a primer on how to boost your lifestyle by introducing elements of European culture to your ordinary life. Kristi has a beautiful, easy to read style.

Bella Figura: How to Live, Love and Eat the Italian Way by Kamin Mohammadi. It's an autobiographical account of how a burnt-out magazine executive moves to Florence and discovers life is full of joy and passion again.

Marie Antoinette by Antonia Fraser. It actually got used as the source material for the Kirsten Dunst/Sofia Copolla movie, but it's a really good book, full of small details, on a life we think we know so much about.

Thomas Cromwell by Tracey Borman. I read this straight after reading Hilary Mantel's books, and it gave me the facts behind the fiction. He was an interesting man.

Wolf Hall and *Bring Up the Bodies* by Hilary Mantel. Just amazing novels. I am desperate for the third part, but I'm thinking Hilary can't bear to kill Tom Crom off. I don't want him to die, either.

Happiness For The Soul:

Happiness is big business at the moment: just google the word and see how many articles, books and sites there are dedicated to keeping us happy. It's right there in the first line of the American Declaration of Independence, the right to Life, Liberty and the Pursuit of Happiness. Perhaps counter-intuitively, I started this book looking at physical ways to boost happiness, at how having a cosy home and a lifestyle set up to promote physical and intellectual wellbeing are integral to happiness. Yet all the happiness actions in the world won't work if you can't feel happy in your soul. Whatever actions you take will be as nothing if your innermost being doesn't balance enough to find that sweet spot where the stresses of the world are handled well enough to leave your soul peaceful and ready to embrace happiness.

This chapter is all about finding ways to slow your soul down, to give yourself the space to think, feel or pray, and the tools to make being happy whatever situation you are in an achievable goal.

Create Your Own Rituals to Restore

Alison May writes online and in her books about homemaking and in her beautifully practical ebook, *The Art of Homemaking*, she writes that

> *"We have to offer ourselves frequent opportunity to renew our*
> *enthusiasm for keeping hearth and home together, remind ourselves*
> *that we are more than homemakers, look after our physical and*
> *emotional wellbeing and keep working on creating the kind of Ministry*
> *to the Beautiful that pays testimony to all our efforts."*

She advises her readers to have a set of personal rituals, physical, mental, emotional and spiritual, that make you feel better and equip you for life ahead.

Whether you work in the home or out of it, taking time for oneself is not selfishness, but self-care. It is well worth working out the very least you need to keep your mind and body together and to mark off the time for that on your calendar before you plan the rest of your life. We're not talking about hours spent in the bath, or weekly manicures. We're talking about taking five or ten minutes here and there, just simple things to bring your mind and body to one place.

You might want to space them out throughout the day: perhaps a cup of lemon tea first thing in the morning, sipped as the sun rises. A short walk at lunchtime listening to a favourite audiobook or podcast. Take five minutes after work or school pickup for a decompression ritual: get changed, or showered after a particularly hard day, lie on your bed and breathe or write in your journal. Make your nighttime ritual comfy cozy: turn down the sheets, spritz with lavender water, make a cup of mild chamomile tea and read a few pages of your book before sliding into sleep.

My rituals are never so perfectly spread. I am quite happy if I only get one or two of these a day, never the full set. I also grab extended time when I can to sit in my hygge nook at home, crocheting, reading or listening to the radio. An hour on a quiet week night spent pleasing just myself is a real blessing in a busy life. I like to do things that centre me, hence the reading or listening rather than watching something.

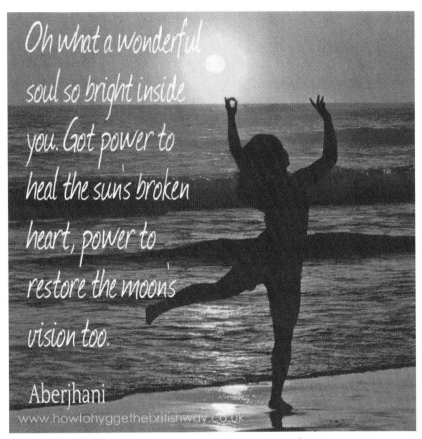

Oh what a wonderful soul so bright inside you. Got power to heal the suns broken heart, power to restore the moons vision too.

Aberjhani

www.howtohyggethebritishway.co.uk

Sometimes I use the time to tidy out a drawer or shelf, so that at the end I can see that my time has improved both mental and physical situation. There is a real link between the state of your mind and the state of your physical surroundings. Even giving the house a darned good clean can be a ritual, if approached correctly, with the best smelling cleaners and household equipment to make you smile.

Action

❖ Look at your day and decide where you most need to start a ritual. Some people find that waking early and having an extra 15 minutes then gives them the boost they need for the rest of the day. As a worker outside of the house, I find my decompression moment when I first come in is invaluable, but if I worked inside the home I might want a 2pm pause, a chance to drink a cup of tea, read or think.

❖ Set out simple rituals that you can keep to. It's no use wanting an hour of solitude and a deep bubble bath every day if, at the moment, having a shower uninterrupted is a blessing. Keep your rituals simple and easily achievable: sipping tea, a shower, or an early bedtime once a week to enjoy the luxury of proper sleep.

❖ Read Alison May's homemaking books. They're available on Kindle and contain hundreds of ideas for making life beautiful. I love her Scrumptious Treats series, and the House series for setting up seasonal rituals that care for you and the house.

Coffee breaks

In Swedish offices, the workers down tools twice a day, mid-morning and mid-afternoon, to share a drink and something sweet. It's called Fika, and it's an excellent way to mark a pause in the work schedule. Anna Brones writes of it that, "Fika isn't just a coffee break, it's a moment to slow down and appreciate the good things in life."[19] I love the idea that the name comes from coffee itself.... Swap the syllables of Kaffe (the Swedish word for coffee) round and you get fika.

The British used to have a great tradition of tea drinking, and tea breaks used to be sacrosanct in places like factories, offices and schools. I'm ashamed to say one school I went into had banned tea breaks in the staff room partly because they wanted the staff all out on the yard patrolling and interacting with the children. Legally in the UK all workers are entitled to 20 minutes break in a six-hour shift, although other breaks are at the discretion of the employer. School said that they didn't pay the workers to sit in the staffroom and talk, and anyway 'some people' were apt to abuse the privilege, so we all had to suffer. Did it make us any better teachers?

---

[19] https://www.thekitchn.com/what-in-the-world-is-fika-an-intro-to-the-swedish-coffee-break-the-art-of-fika-219297

In Sweden, coffee is something to look forward to, a moment where everything else stops and you savour the moment.

Anna Brones

I know the school lost out on a valuable source of communication. If the only time you ever see a colleague is as you pass by their door on the way in or out, if the only time you ask about their day is as the day ends, then the chances of building strong bonds of professional friendship remain low. And when the chalk-face staff saw the very same office staff that had told them there was 'no opportunity for a break during the day' taking regular tea or coffee breaks, all be it at their desks and not around the staff room, morale wasn't likely to be high at what they saw as a hypocritical attitude to recuperation.

Taking a break with others from work is a way to build relationships. Sharing small snippets of problems, little issues that you're struggling with, is a good way to find that either they aren't really problems, except in your perception and you can re-frame them, or there are others with the same issues and you can work together to solve it. Sharing personal information selectively and getting to know people as work friends as well as colleagues will also give you an insight into why certain people are as they are. The family dynamics for a mother of three with a husband who works away will be different than those of the single person in their twenties who lives a lively life. Having compassion for and an understanding of external pressures doesn't mean you have to 'let people off work' because of them, but does mean you may understand the late start after a bad night that the new father pulls once or twice that first month.

"It's this intention to slow down and take a break that makes it such an important part of daily life -- one that not only connects people by opening up windows to decompress and communicate, but because it's a shared value -- a tradition recognized as important throughout the country."

Anna Brones

Not a worker in an external situation? Okay, you work from home. You can still build fika into your life. Arrange to meet a friend for coffee sometimes, make your own drink and scroll through your favourite groups on Facebook, or even just sit and write a letter to an absent friend. My retired parents have finally learned the value of fika. Every day at 3 they down tools as long as they are at home, make a cup of coffee or tea and each eat two gingernut biscuits... never more... as they pause in their life and enjoy a quiet moment.

Action

❖ Build a pause into your working day, whether you are in an office or at home. On days when everybody is home, it can be good to make a cake and call them around to eat together.

❖ When the Huffpost is extolling the virtues of fika, it's worth trying to make it a part of the office culture.[20] Productivity studies show that Sweden has one of the highest rates of productivity even though they have a culture that expects shorter working hours and breaks.... Some would say the productivity is because of the

---

[20] http://www.huffingtonpost.co.uk/entry/swedish-coffee-break_n_7033082

hours and breaks. If you know you have to finish at 4pm, you will work harder to get everything done. Try working Swedish for a week. Worktime is worktime and breaktime is breaktime.

❖ Need inspiration? Read *Fika: The Art of the Swedish Coffee Break* by Anna Brones and Johanna Kindvall. It has several excellent recipes for traditional Swedish cakes and pastries, as well as explaining why fika holds such a place in the hearts of the Swedes.

Working Out a Work/Life balance

I work with my husband: he's a lovely man, as I've said before and will say again. Working for him is not a burden, it's work I enjoy in a location I find enjoyable (I get regular cups of tea and a view out over a McDonalds restaurant) but I have to make sure it gets balanced against the other areas of my life.

Before Christmas 2017 I was working 9 to 5 most days in the office and then coming home to another hour or two of tutoring before making tea and cleaning the house. I had a very bad work-life balance. I hadn't seen my Mum and Dad in a while, and I was feeling guilty about that. I had begun cancelling evening events because the pressures were getting to me and I was too tired to go out, and I felt ill. Something had to give.

Fortunately working for the husband makes approaching the Boss to discuss working situation a lot easier. We agreed that the best present I could give my parents was actually my time, so we arranged that, appointments allowing, I would take Tuesday afternoons off from lunchtime and alleviate my guilt about the parents. Now I go every Tuesday and enjoy either sitting talking, or taking Mum out for coffee and a browse in a shop.

I looked at the house. I am not a minimalist, but I can appreciate that a tidy house is easier to clean. I decided to involve the other people in the house. I write a chores list and we all do the chores we are best at. That means most washing is done by my daughter, a lot of polishing and hoovering is done by the sons and we all change our own beds. Taking a lot of the housework out of the evening's chore list has given me time to relax as well.

Working hard for something we don't care about is called stress: Working hard for something we love is called passion.

Simon Sinek

www.howtohyggethebritishway.co.uk

If you're working at a job that demands every bit of your time, you need to work out cheat systems, ways to make the rest of your life easier. Perhaps you can combine exercise and friendship by going to the gym or a class with a friend? Use time management techniques to work smarter not longer and find shortcuts to make your job easier. Perhaps using checklists on mundane and repetitive elements will free your brain so that you can use it for the more creative parts of your job. *The Checklist Manifesto* by Atul Gawande is all about how the author, a doctor, uses checklists all the time to speed up working practices, ensure safety and increase productivity. If you can remove some of the more mundane tasks that take up thoughtspace, it can help to relieve stress a little and leave your brain power free for more important things.

Work/life balance is a very personal issue. You may totally love your job and see no problems in spending your weekends doing it: or you have children at home and see every minute away from them as a minute wasted making money not love. It will also change as time goes by, so what makes for a good work life balance now may feel unbalanced at a later time. Be adaptable, and do what suits you now, not what suits others.[21]

Action

❖ Most books on work-life balance are written from the point of view of office workers. You may be better looking for a guru in real life. Look around and see if there's anyone in your immediate workplace or friendship circle who seems to have their life balanced. Ask them how they do it and consider using any good advice they give you.

❖ Ultimately your work-life balance only has to suit you. Be adaptable, and accept that a balanced life this month may need tweaking next month.

❖ The Swedish concept of Lagom is big on work-life balance. Read a couple of the most recent books out to see what advice they give that you can choose and adapt. I particularly recommend *Live Lagom* by Anna Brones and *Lagom* by Linnea Dunne. Sadly, the Swedes don't believe in working late while the UK and the USA do. It may be that you need to show that effective working doesn't need to take all your time, and set the example for others to follow.

What are your simple pleasures?

In *Simple Abundance*, Sarah Ban Breathnach outlines a list of Joyful Simplicities for each month of the year. When I was a new mother, 20 years ago, I found these lists were a useful way of exploring what made me happier as a person. I would read each list at the start of the month and choose perhaps only one or two that I wanted to get done or knew I could get done in the month. They were seasonal, so bulb planting happened in autumn, while egg decorating happened in spring. I liked that seasonal touch, but I also needed a list that didn't alter with the weather.

[2121] https://www.mentalhealth.org.uk/a-to-z/w/work-life-balance

That was when I first drew up my own list of simple pleasures. The small, cheap things I could do, often taking less than 10 minutes, but occasionally needing a real investment of time. I loved that having the list with me in my planner meant I was never at a loss for something to do to please me.

Sometimes, the simple things are more fun and meaningful than all the banquets in the world.

E.A. Bucchianeri

www.howtohyggethebritishway.co.uk

And I have kept a list in my planner ever since. I call it my Bliss List now, a short (or long) list of the things that I know make me happier if I make time for them in my life. The coffee with a friend, the reading of a chapter of a good book, watching a never-fail programme or movie. Things that I can do alone or with a special friend, in the house or out. If it's an activity that I know usually leaves me feeling calmer, more at peace, happier or otherwise beneficially affected, then it goes on my bliss list.

Take a few moments now to begin your list. Turn to a clean page and jot down things that you know make you happy, or at least restore your equilibrium.

We're not after things that take hours or need a million and one resources here: the point about simple pleasures is that they are easy enough to do without needing the stress of shopping or too much planning ahead. They should also suit you and you alone: miss off the garden centre visit you make to please your mother or the football game you watch to please your partner. These only need to suit you. Everyone's bliss list will be different, so don't judge or compare. You can, however, borrow ideas off others. Just add them to your list and they are yours.

Here, to start you off, is my current bliss list in my planner:

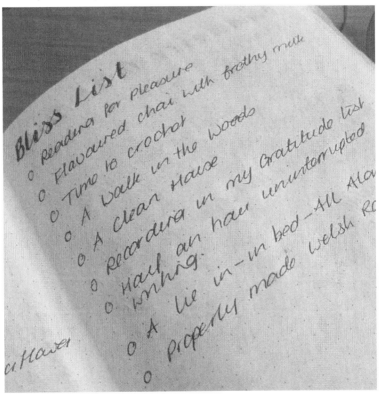

They are really small things, can you see? I try to have a blissful moment at least once a day… I know when I'm being too hard on myself because these small pleasures are often the first ones to go. I also know friends who say they feel guilty about taking time out for themselves and I say: **don't feel guilt**. Never. Just remember the oxygen mask metaphor. If you don't look after yourself, how will you be fit to look after others?

Action:

❖ Start a list for yourself of the small actions that give you pleasure. Keep it in a planner or a notebook so that you can look at it often and add to it as often as you like.

❖ Do something off the list, something little but often. And do it without guilt, because you need to do these little things for your own good.

❖ The Simple Things have a Could do list for each month, a really easy idea that several bloggers have taken to imitating. Just search 'Could Do List' for more inspiration.

❖ You do have a copy of *Simple Abundance*, don't you? Along with the sensuous *Romancing The Ordinary*, it gives you seasonal advice on making your life beautiful and becoming the best You that you can be.

Find your flow activity

Have you ever sat down to do something for just five minutes, only to look up after a short length of time and find that the afternoon or evening has flown away on you? Time has been lost, passed very beautifully in an activity that took up all your attention and left you in a place apart from this world where moments blend together and nothing pulled you back to reality?

I've been like that when drawing or painting, sometimes. It's good to get lost in the creative process, to be so all-consumed in making or doing that, really, you could just sit and do it all day. I know good musicians will lose track of time as well. I love music, but I'm no skilled musician. As a teenager I loved a passage from *Dragonsinger: Harper of Pern* by Anne McCaffrey. Menolly is a musician, and when she goes to the Harperhall she gets to play with other, far more skilled, musicians. Playing for the first time in a quartet she felt

"the stimulation of playing with three keen and competent musicians
gave her such impulsion that she seemed to be an irrelevant
medium for fingers that had to play what her eager eyes saw. She
was lost completely in the thrall of the music, so that when the
rushing finale ended, she suffered a shock as complete as pain.

The idea of losing time doing something one loves and is good at is called flow. Recognised and named by Mihaly Csikszentmihalyi in his book, *Flow: The Psychology of Happiness*, flow is what happens when the challenge of the activity and the skill level we have match and produce a perfect moment when time ceases to matter.

Flow requires us to be active, and to have spent time working hard to achieve a level of skill. Like Menolly in the quote above, we have to be proficient enough to take on the challenge without being daunted. Sport, art, craft, music and work can all be paths to find your flow. In a darker way, gambling and video games can be flow activities, so flow cannot always be seen as a force for good.

In terms of creating happiness, flow is a good thing to work towards. It is capable of strengthening our sense of self after the experience although during the activity we may well lose self-consciousness for a time. It produces enjoyment, pride in an achievement and a sense of control.

Flow may be a state of ultimate enjoyment, but it does require work and effort to begin with. It can take 10,000 hours of practicing an activity to become an expert, and sometimes recognizing the activity that you are really good at requires openness to trying new things. That's why I'm a middling musician and a cracking craftswoman. I never enjoyed the mundane practicing of scales and arpeggios that create skill, but the fiddling with hooks, needles and knitting pins suited me far more. Do I regret it? Somedays. It's easier to find ways to make music in a group than to find a set of crafters happy to sit in flow together. But what is life, if we never regret anything?

Action

- ❖ Identify your flow activity. Are you an expert yet? Then keep practicing. Don't be afraid to change your mind to find the activity that suits you best.
- ❖ Don't go chasing the flow feeling. That doesn't work. Just identify it and appreciate it when it happens to you.
- ❖ Use that memory to build your happiness at a later date when you need it. Remembering how a past moment made you feel can build your self-resilience in a tough spot in the future.

Schedule time for you that is sacred

Everybody is entitled to some time when nobody is talking to them and they can just be. That's far easier to write than to achieve.

When I was the mother of three children with only four years between top and bottom child, there were days when everything I did was accompanied by one child, if I was lucky, or by a trio of talking, attention-intensive children. It's not that they were attention seeking, more that they enjoyed paying attention to what I was up to, even if that was going to the toilet or cleaning out a cupboard. And at that time, mindful that the day would come when I wasn't the Centre of their World (and how!) I rode out the feeling of never being alone and took my quantum of solitude when I could.

Solitude is pleasant. Loneliness is not.

Anna Neagle

www.howtohyggethebritishway.co.uk

I need time alone. I can't function well if I am in constant communication with people, either physically or virtually. I love solitude, time to think or do or just be. Unscheduled free time to read or walk or write. I always have needed to be able to go apart and create. When I was a teenager, my Mother's favourite comment was that I would nest in my bedroom for hours, like the night owl I was, only coming down to eat or watch my favourite TV programmes. I was happy, though, and creative, so she didn't worry much about me. Remember, these were the pre-internet days when I wouldn't have been able to connect with the outside world anyway. I just needed to be alone to write or draw without interruptions. I did my best work alone.

Science backs up my need for solitude as a restorative power as well. Research from a science collective called Hubub[22] and from Finland[23] both show that time spent alone is the best way to rest and get energy back.

Solitude doesn't mean loneliness: it's a positive state of happiness with oneself. It's being free to spend the time doing something for oneself. And we all need to find time to do it, whether we grab our solitude at home, in work or have to go somewhere else. Getting your head together, being free to feel happy, needs you to be able to spend time with yourself without feeling guilty or thinking you should be anywhere else.

Action:

❖ Find some time every week to do something or nothing just for you. Schedule it in and keep it as a sacred engagement. It could be a lunchtime, a half hour on the drive home or time at home when you lock the bedroom door and do whatever gives you pleasure.

❖ Parents or caregivers have problems: very often even finding a space to do something 'just for you' can be impossible if children are very young or your charge needs constant care. It might feel awkward, but ask for help. Even just swapping a playdate with a friend in a similar situation and grabbing 30 minutes every other week is better than nothing. Or set strict bedtimes and grab your chance then.

❖ Use the time well. Doing nothing is better than doing the housework, but a sudden blast of freedom may hit you unprepared. Keep a list of five-minute solitude-requiring activities that you could do: reading, sleeping, crafting, walking, watching old movies, sipping tea etc.... or if you enjoy the meditation in gardening or housework, then do it, but it must be a pleasure not a task.

---

[22] http://hubbubresearch.org/rest-test-results/

[23] https://goo.gl/TQ7sE3

- ❖ Don't let someone else dictate what you should do with your time off. Any errands or 'could you just…' will wait for another time. This is YOUR time, and to spend it doing something involuntarily would destroy the purpose. Keep it sacred FOR YOU.

Get Outside For Some of the Best Medicine

For much of this book I know I sound like I hated teaching and schools, I keep pointing out the wrong in it. And it's true that there is much about school life that I hated by the end, but there is one part of the school day that I really enjoyed. Playtime.

For at least 20 minutes most days I had to stand on a playground walking and talking to children. When I was a supply teacher, playground duty was almost automatically issued as another task, even (in one school) on days when I knew it wasn't actually the teacher I was covering's day, while in my last school, adults all stood out to foster relationships and encourage sensible play. The days when I covered the Early Years like Reception and Nursery I could spend a lot of time outside. I loved it. Sunshine is beneficial, while fresh air clears the cobwebs and makes thinking easier. Add to that the fact that watching younger children explore the big new world around them is a wonderful and very grounding experience, and they were some of the best days of my life.

We can learn much about enjoying the benefits of nature from children. Firstly, they tend not to see weather as good or bad, just different. As long as they have a good coat, or even without, they're happy to go out whatever the weather. In the depths of winter, just 20 minutes of sunshine adds to our Vitamin D… the happiness vitamin… and we need to get out there and uncover our arms as much as we can.

Children don't need toys with batteries to enjoy their time outside, and neither do we. Leave the phone at home sometimes, rather than automatically listening to music or a podcast. Or set yourself a limit: "I will walk to the park with my headphones on and then sit and listen to the sounds around me". How will you ever hear the Woodpecker, if you never let him speak to you?

Adopt the
pace of nature:
her secret
is patience.

Ralph Waldo Emerson

Getting out also means we meet people. Have you ever watched a young child make a connection with someone? Firstly, they make eye contact, then they smile, then they talk. Talking to people is the most nerve-wracking thing for some people, but I love it. I love knowing who, what and why. I'm not afraid to ask, either. What's the worst that can happen? They get sniffy and move away? That's their loss. They ask questions? Well, if I'm happy to ask, I'm happy to tell. Especially if I meet them on a regular route or at a regular time, then it makes sense to build a rapport so that the next time you meet there's always a smile and a word. That's how kindness spreads.

My big outdoor plan this year is in my newly-tidied front garden. We have finally cleared the bins from the side of the garage (the front of the house) to the proper side of the house. I've now got a wide and clear path that passes by my Hygge Nook room. It's beautifully just wide enough for a bench, and that's what I'm saving up for now. A proper park bench, strong and sturdy. I want to sit out most evenings, sipping my tea, watching the world go by and greeting my neighbours, old and new.

Action:

- ❖ Do you have a local park? Plan regular trips to it and grow to know and love the sounds you hear there.
- ❖ Get outside in the sunshine for 20 minutes a day all year round. Even if it's only a walk at lunchtime, as long as you are in the sun with some skin exposed you will feel the benefit. Leave your gloves off, or pull up your sleeves a little. I like to walk in a thick jumper and scarf, rather than a coat, when possible. It keeps my neck warm, but lets me expose my arms.
- ❖ Do you have an outdoor seating area? Even just an old dining chair put in a sunny area can be enough. Sit and enjoy the sun whenever you can.

Forest Bathing: Why Trees are more beneficial than we realize

We have a patch of woodland near our house called Childwall Woods. I've written about it before, in my *Summer Hygge book*. It's a beautiful 39-acre patch of woodland and wilderness, with paths through the trees and across scrubland. It's only 100 yards from a couple of the busiest roads in Liverpool, but it's an oasis of calm every time we enter it. And I swear I leave the place feeling more relaxed every time I go. Simply walking through the trees has a positive effect on me, always has done ever since I was 13 and decided I was really an elf (I have a very long-standing love affair with *The Lord of The Rings*: I was either an elf, or a shieldmaiden. Best of all, I thought, would be to be an elven shieldmaiden. A bit like Tauriel the Elf that they added to the over-whelmingly masculine Hobbit films). I have always loved to be surrounded by trees. You might almost say, I love to be immersed in them. In Japan, they love it as well. They call it Forest bathing.

Forest bathing is called Shinrin Yoku in Japanese, and it's been a part of the Government's health programme there since 1982. It has scientifically proven benefits for mental health and immune system function[24]. It lowers stress levels, calms the spirit and reduces hostility. The aim is not to set off anywhere, or to do anything, but to meander and be immersed in the sights, sounds and smell of the forest. Even as little as 15 minutes has an impact on your wellbeing.

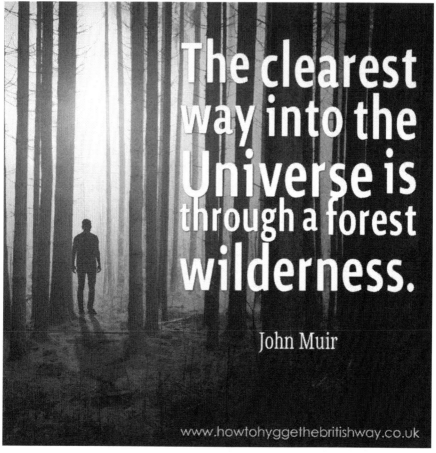

The clearest way into the Universe is through a forest wilderness.

John Muir

www.howtohyggethebritishway.co.uk

You can go alone or with others, but what is crucial is that none of you are connected to anything electrical. No phones, no music players, nothing that needs a battery. Just you and your lungs and the forest. Walk in peace, admire the trees and bathe in the relaxing beauty and positive benefits.

---

[24] https://qz.com/804022/health-benefits-japanese-forest-bathing/

Action:

❖ Identify your favourite local forest or woodland. If you're lucky, you'll have a small space within a short walk, otherwise you will need to drive and find the nearest one available.

❖ Be safe: always make sure someone knows where you are, especially if you're visiting the woods alone. You may want to take your phone with you, but leave it in your pocket.

❖ Fascinated by the wildlife you've seen? You may be able to recognise them using a website like www.woodlandtrust.org.uk or a simple book such as *The Usborne Spotter's Guide to Woodland Life*, which is a children's book, but very informative.

❖ Can't get to a wood? Then just sit outside anywhere green, and breathe in the sights and sounds that you can see there.

Find Your Creative Path

I have a wonderful sister in law, who can dance, sing and play the piano and clarinet. She is such a musical person that when I needed a musical interlude during the register signing at my wedding, I asked Jane to play Mozart's Clarinet Concerto, just the middle movement. It was sublime.

Having a friend like that is intimidating. I might be a really good musician, but if I compare myself to Jane, I feel like an absolute beginner. I never even considered pushing my musical abilities in school because I know I'm not as good as she is. Comparisons are odious, and that's a pain. If we will only do something as long as we can be the best: well, you won't be doing much because there is always someone better than you at anything, be it creating, driving, speaking French, cleaning the house or growing dahlias. Fact.

Yet if we are prepared to do things even if we know we won't be the best or the most wonderful or even be any good at first, we will learn so much more from a position of ignorance than ever we do from a position of expertise. The surprise of finding out we are wrong triggers the brain into remembering. When we start to learn, we are not seeking perfection, we are seeking to be good enough.

Personality begins where comparison leaves off. Be unique. Be memorable. Be confident. Be proud.

Shannon L. Alder

Not everybody can be an artist: not everybody can sing and very few people will ever achieve the skill level in dance needed to appear at the Royal Ballet. Don't be put off by that: everybody can be creative, even if in a prosaic way. Finding your creative path is about finding the thing that you can do that will make you feel creative. It's about pushing outside of your comfort zone, about trying out things that aren't your flow activities (remember, we talked about those earlier in this chapter) and learning to be a learner again. The advantages of starting new stuff at any age are that our brain gets stretched, we learn new skills that may be transferable, it encourages our problem-solving skills and we get the benefit of doing something that may... or may not... become a new flow activity. And the advantage of creative learning is that it stimulates different parts of your brain from those that working, talking and daily life use.

Try out a few creative hobbies, either by collecting the resources and self-learning or by taking a class or short course. You don't want to sign up for a long and expensive course if this hobby works out to not be up your street or you know you want to try something else as well. Take evening classes, which are usually available at a local school or college and come in a wide range of subjects, or find a mentor. If you're a crafter and have always been a crafter, try a slightly different course, such as woodwork or metal work. I am still aiming to get on a pottery course before I'm too much older... and an upholstery course, a woodworking course and a dress-making course.

Look around to find the stranger or more unique course run by small independent creators. Is there a glass-blowing course or an ironwork course you could go on? Or become an apprentice to an expert in the field.

Some activities are best taught in small groups or individually. Learning a musical instrument can be easier and cheaper in a group of 2 or 3 if the price of individual lessons is too steep. Or if price is too great for you to pay, ask a musical friend to start you off before you decide to invest in the full cost.

Action

- ❖ Make a skills wish list. Put down all the things you could ever be interested in doing, and then narrow it down to your top three or four.
- ❖ Look out for classes in local papers and on local websites. You may find knows of a course of class as well.
- ❖ Don't invest in the gear at first. You want to be sure this is a craft/activity for you before you do. Borrow from friends and try it for a while first, before you invest.

You are not responsible for anyone else

Have you ever been out with someone who has misbehaved and made a holy show of you? It's embarrassing, and I have often sat wishing the ground would swallow me up while a child throws a tantrum for something that I have been mean enough to say no to. You know, like the large chocolate bar just before dinner, the big toy in the toyshop or wanting to run out in the road. The worst ones of all are when you take a child to a restaurant or enclosed space and they throw the tantrum, in full view of everyone and cause people to look and either nod in brotherhood or tsk in censure. Like I can help the tantrum happening.

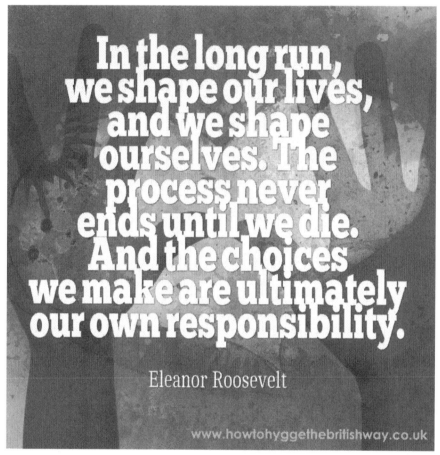

In the long run, we shape our lives, and we shape ourselves. The process never ends until we die. And the choices we make are ultimately our own responsibility.

Eleanor Roosevelt

www.howtohyggethebritishway.co.uk

Well, I felt like that with the first child. Whatever he did reflected on me. He's crying? It must be my fault. Throwing a tantrum? I haven't done something I was supposed to. I felt like everything about this small human being was supposed to be in my control and I could change his mood.

It took me only a little time with a toddler to realise that anything more like an uncontrollable force of nature than a child between the age of 1 and 3 cannot be imagined. I could steer, but I couldn't control. By the time my second child had come along I knew that the bad days they had were not my fault. I no longer apologized for their misbehaviour. I would do my best, but failure wasn't a failure for me. It was a failure of my child's undeveloped social skills. I pinned my hopes on them growing up and growing responsible. I modelled good behaviour, rewarded them when they behaved, refused to shift for tantrums over 'Me Want'-ies and spoke always with patience and love.

I love taking my young adults out now, but I am more likely to be the 'nodding in brotherhood' than tsk at the toddlers I see now. I just wish I could tell the parents that this time, like all others, will pass, and they're doing well.

You are also not responsible for the emotions of other people. Unless you have done something to create bad feelings, you cannot claim responsibility for another person's bad feelings.

The takeaway point of this chapter is this: You are not responsible for how other people behave or feel. You are not responsible for your Mum, partner, child, office colleague or whomever usually lets themselves down in public. Release that stress, refuse to apologise for other's mistakes and move on gracefully.

You are your own person: owning your own mistakes should be enough. You need to own up to those, apologise when you make mistakes and move on.

Action

- ❖ Work on telling yourself that you are not responsible for other people's actions. Say it under your breath, write it on a post-it, paint it on a wall.
- ❖ Struggling with parent guilt when your children misbehave? Share the story with another parent.... You will never be the only one going through this, so speak up and share! And let the child learn that they are responsible for how they behave. It's a long time since I was the mother of toddlers, but the best advice given to me then was (and still is) **choose your battles**. Not everything is worth World War 3 about.
- ❖ Accept responsibility for yourself, and then learn to forgive. This can be hard, but it's worth doing again and again. You're a human being, you're not perfect.

Not all darkness is frightening

Were you scared of the dark when you were little? Snuggled up in my bed, with my teddy bear and the sounds of the family home all around me, I don't remember feeling a particular fear of the dark there. I do remember feeling scared when I was older, camping in a tent in the middle of a forested camp site and a trip to the toilet was a long walk through trees full of sounds. I think I tested my bladder that weekend, rather than set off alone in the dark.

Of course, nothing was going to happen to me on the walk to the toilet: it was a Scout campsite and, as far as possible, the only people on it were Cubs and their Leaders (including me: I was actually Akela at that point!) and in the cold light of day I would tell you that. The night has a strange effect on our reasoning.

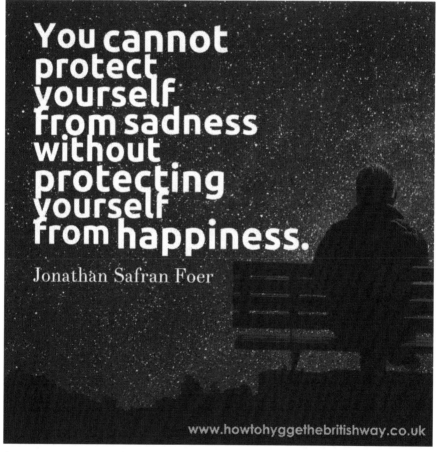

You cannot protect yourself from sadness without protecting yourself from happiness.

Jonathan Safran Foer

www.howtohyggethebritishway.co.uk

An even worse darkness is that of the spirit when we get low. Worry about life, a change in circumstances, illness, assuming responsibility for things we can't change... they all have the potential to take us to a dark place. I know when I was desperate for a child after trying for a year that I got myself into a very dark spot. I couldn't look at a baby without crying, I found myself feeling angry at other people's happy announcements, and every month my period fell like a black cloud across my sky. I recognised the darkness around me, but didn't know how to cope.

My make or break moment came when the neighbour next door knocked and said she was pregnant... and that she hadn't even been trying. It was like a slap in the face. I smiled at her, and closed the door, and sat down weeping.

I think that was the darkest moment of that time. It was seriously unfair. There we were, trying and desperate, and there she was just getting knocked up without a care in the world. I could have stayed in my pit of despair and let myself get buried by the darkness. I could have fallen out with my lovely neighbor, hated the baby and spent my time begrudging every moment of his life. I was very fortunate that my brain at that time was resilient. I boxed up the sadness, washed my face and set course for a new and different future. Basically, I talked myself back into a better place. I wasn't getting pregnant? Well, perhaps there was a reason for it. Perhaps I would never get pregnant, in which case, what was I prepared to do about it?

I started planning alternate universes. I set a date to visit the Doctor and started to push for investigations. I set aside some extra money every month for IVF, if we were going to need it, and I looked at my future career plans. If there were going to be no babies in my life, then I would put my creative and emotional energies into a job I loved. I signed up for an M.Ed, read books like there was no tomorrow and started planning my progression from English Coordinator to Deputy to....

Well, I fell pregnant roughly eighteen months later. I think accepting the situation and releasing my tension had a lot to do with it. Stress has a strong effect on the body, and a stressed body doesn't always behave. Having reached my low point, and accepted the darkness, it was my role in life to find a way out of the woods. But that period in my life gave me some great benefits. I can still think how horrible my infertility (even if only for a short time actually) felt, so I have great sympathy for those who are in that plight. I know how easily an issue can come between family and friends. I also know how necessary it is to get past that darkness and to head towards the light. Sometimes our path in life is not the one we thought we would be treading: be strong, set your course, and lay hold of the tiller. Be resilient, focus on your happiness and be happy with what you have.

Action:

❖ If you are in a dark place, and no amount of happiness talking will get you out of it, please go and ask for help. Phone someone, see the doctor, tell another person about your worries.

❖ For mild depression, or a temporary period of unhappiness, try www.mind.org.uk for some good advice. It's basically common sense: eat well, sleep well and connect with others. Remember the good times and ask for help when you need it.

❖ *How to Be Human: The Manual* by Ruby Wax with a neuroscientist and a monk is one of my favourite books on mindfulness, happiness and how to survive as a human.

Collect memories not things

When it comes to keeping my mind clear, I find (like a lot of people) that there is a close relationship between how my house looks and how my mind works. If my house is packed with stuff, cluttered and untidy, my mind eventually becomes paralysed. It stops thinking clearly and can't get much beyond thinking about the state of the sink.

Now I am a dreadful shop addict. I will always love going into shops, especially household-y shops full of bargains, and browsing along the rails and shelves looking for the one Big Bargain that is waiting for me. I do this with home accessories, shoes, bags, books and pretty much anything you care to mention. Once upon a time, I couldn't get out of the place without buying something.

Do you remember Woolworths? When the children were young, I would visit once or twice a week. If I was lucky there would be a reason for my purchase, like we needed lightbulbs or a new washing up brush. If there wasn't a reason, I promise you we would probably come out with something anyway. A toy, a book, some clothes, some socks, a VHS tape (at that time)… and my house was filled with crap. Not quality items, but cheap plastic tat.

Holidays were no exception. My husband said it was like I had a terrible souvenir shop addiction, any and everything was fair game. I could visit a museum or village and spend half an hour in the shop, buying a pencil or a pad or a coaster. Anything that caught my eye. It wasn't a good use of time or resources, and over the years my house was becoming cramped with geegaws that took up space, needed dusting and meant nothing.

What happened to stop me? I have no real idea: I can only think that my interest in minimalism happened. When the children were still at primary school, I started a blog, and went searching for other blogs. As well as Brocante Home, which fed my whimsical side, I found Zen Habits and Becoming Minimalist. They were talking about leading a full life with less stuff, about living to enjoy not to acquire.

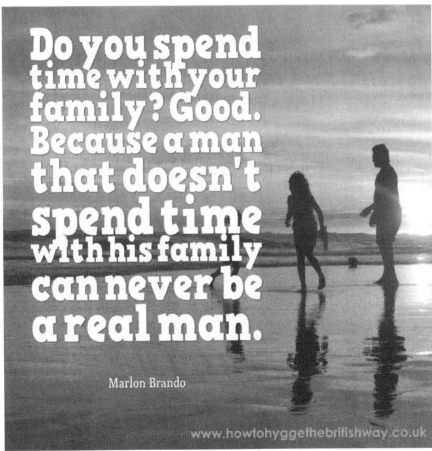

Do you spend time with your family? Good. Because a man that doesn't spend time with his family can never be a real man.

Marlon Brando

www.howtohyggethebritishway.co.uk

It's taken me years, and I am far from a minimalist. I buy carefully, I select good stuff that I know I need rather than want. I have a 30-day cooling off period on big purchases, and I shop around for the best value and quality mix. I also keep a shopping list in my planner where I note down things I've noticed that we need, whether that's clothes or household items, and I stick to that list.

I'd say my big downfall is handbags (one can never have too many bags, really) and I still have a habit of buying a small souvenir from places I visit, although nowadays it's either a Christmas ornament, which I mark with place and year and then display every Christmas on the family tree, or it's a snow globe that sits on a shelf with the rest, beautifully lit by fairy lights. Both of them are really like aide-memoires to special moments or experiences and give me pleasure and a warm feeling when I look at them.

My money nowadays is spent on experiences, saved up for holidays or used for theatre and cinema trips. My children are aged 20 to 16. I won't have them at home much longer, and I want to spend time with them. Investing in experiences gives them, and me, a focus outside of each other and makes evenings a pleasure, rather than a chore (for them).

Action:

❖ Focus on decluttering things that don't give you pleasure. Your house should be filled with personal items that arouse memories in you and surround you with love and happiness.

❖ Money spent on activities will always be money well spent. Research shows that we will feel happier about the money spent, that the memory of the event boosts our happiness levels and that the anticipation, experience and memory of an experience gives us a three-fold increase in happiness.

When life gives you lemons... adjust your attitude

Bad things happen. That's a fact of life. Life is an imperfect experience designed to end for everyone only one way: in death.

But how we see our path towards our inevitable conclusion can make a big difference to our happiness on that path. We have a powerful weapon on our side, capable of taking obstacles and issues that could floor another person and making them into challenges and opportunities for us to handle, overcome, and stride past.

It's called your brain. And overwriting the negative track with a positive attitude and approach to living is called cognitive reframing.

We all have a brain, and internalized voices telling us how we feel, what we did wrong, what our faults are. It's easy to listen to it, and to agree "Yes, that was stupid. Grief, I shouldn't have done that. Oh No! I have that happening tomorrow: I'll be judged by the rest of the class, I'm bound to slip up, I'll never be any good...." Our internal track is often hardwired to give us the worst criticism. Let's blame it on evolution: the animal aware of the most problems and dangers is the animal most likely to survive. For many people, it's the result of past trauma or experiences. We look at a thing and see the negative, the work necessary, the problems.

Breaking out of that cycle of thinking takes work and determination, which you must have. You've made it this far in my book, you've definitely got persistence! It's a two-step process:

1. Observe your negative thoughts.
2. Replace them with positive ones.[25]

Observing your thoughts can be as organised as writing them down when you become aware of them, to wearing a wrist band made of elastic and snapping it against your wrist when you know you're being negative. It stops the negative thoughts in their tracks and makes you aware of how often you bad-mouth yourself.

Replacing bad thoughts with good needs you to be adaptable. You will be identifying your negative thoughts and then adapting them. Use less extreme language; mildly dislike something rather than hate it. Change the internal wording from 'That's a problem', to 'that's a challenge' and ask 'What's the best way to deal with this?'. You are letting yourself know that there are multiple options in life: that you can choose the best option for you at this moment. If you find life is giving you lemons, perhaps it's time to become a greengrocer? Fix a gin and tonic with a slice, make lemon drizzle cake, use the lemon to clean the handles in the house. A problem like too many lemons is easy to solve, when you put your brain to work on it.

For an easy and practical book on this, try *Reframe Your Viewpoints* by Virginia Ritterbusch. It's a short, easy read about challenging and changing your inner voice.

---

[25] http://feelhappiness.com/reframing-your-thoughts-make-yourself-happier/

I believe that if life gives you lemons, you should make lemonade ... And try to find somebody whose life has given them vodka, and have a party.

Ron White

www.howtohyggethebritishway.co.uk

Action:

❖ The way you approach a challenge will decide whether that challenge is good or bad. Your mind has the ability to turn an obstacle into an opportunity. Start now, by listing 5 issues you have and then reframing them as positives. Use the advice in the article listed to help you. Use positive words like 'Challenge', 'Opportunity' or 'Strengths'

❖ Identify your own weaknesses and turn them into strengths. Are you indecisive? That means you take your time before making a decision. Get angry very quickly? You're passionate about what concerns you. Your faults may also be your best features.

Find your mottoes and use them well

The right word of advice at the right time can be just the jolt you need to break out of a dip and climb back into the sun. During my last year at school I felt close to breaking point and went looking for a quote about how the strongest rock could be broken down by the rain. Instead I found a quotation on the creation of diamonds.

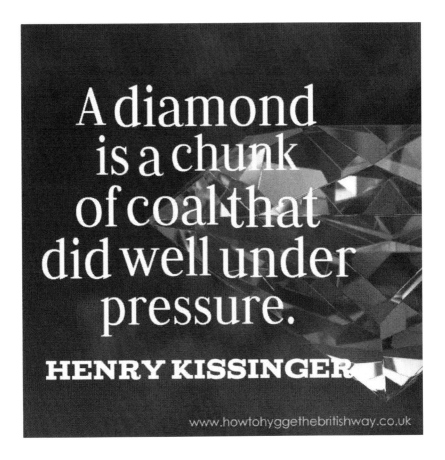

A diamond is a chunk of coal that did well under pressure.

HENRY KISSINGER

www.howtohyggethebritishway.co.uk

It was just what I needed at that time: to know that the pressure I was feeling didn't need to break me and crack me; but could help me become stronger and a better person (see what I mean about reframing issues to make them a positive) and I used this quote to keep me strong.

If you follow my blog, How to Hygge the British Way, or any of my social media streams you will know that I love quotations. I like finding the right words to sum up a feeling, or a moment in my life. The right quotation will give you strength, will remind you that you are not alone or will give you the permission you need to be yourself at that moment, whether that is a crying mess in the corner or a Valkyrie riding roughshod over the opponents (and you may veer between one and the other. Quotes give you permission to do that as well).

I love having them at my disposal. When I see one that speaks to me I save it, either to a Word document or in my bullet journal, and when I am at a loose end and at the computer I use a quotation maker programme to make a jpeg that is shareable and ready to go on my blog or feeds.

If you're not great with IT, or time is limited, then a quick search of Pinterest for inspirational quotes will give you a whole range of wise words from ancient times to modern days.

A fine quotation is a diamond in the hand of a man of wit and a pebble in the hand of a fool.

Joseph Roux

www.howtohyggethebritishway.co.uk

All the quotes from my books, blog and social media are available on Pinterest in a board named How to Hygge The British Way Quotes. They're available for use free, although my one request is that you don't edit the blog link off the bottom.

Action

❖ Collect the quotes that speak to you. Start a Pinterest board, computer folder or simply print out and stick up where you can see them often. And change them often as well; our eyes get very used to wallpaper on the walls and on the computer very quickly so changing the quotes you see will encourage you to look at them and learn them.

❖ Good sources for quotes are Brainy Quote and Goodreads. If you have a particular topic you need a quote about, enter the keyword and see what turns up.

❖ Use a daily quote app for inspiration every day. I like Inspirational Quotes, which has a good variety of quotes to access on the phone.

Happiness For the Soul Resources

Websites and Articles

http://www.thesimplethings.com/search?q=could%20do&f_collectionId=5461dbf9e4b0bc6861f691a3 The search page for all their Could Do pages on the blog. The whole site is full of ideas and illustrations to fire up your enthusiasm.

https://www.thekitchn.com/what-in-the-world-is-fika-an-intro-to-the-swedish-coffee-break-the-art-of-fika-219297 Anna Brones introduction to Fika, and why it's so useful to the Swedes.

http://positivepsychology.org.uk/living-in-flow/ Looking at flow: the article sums up the basics you need to recognise flow in your life, plus positive and negative aspects.

http://www.dailyshoring.com/flow-activities/ A short list of some activities that the writer knows may help you find your flow.

https://www.psychologytoday.com/blog/high-octane-women/201201/6-reasons-you-should-spend-more-time-alone Reasons why we should spend time alone, if you needed any.

https://qz.com/804022/health-benefits-japanese-forest-bathing/ About the medicinal side of forest bathing, and how it helps restore mind and body.

www.woodlandtrust.org.uk Information on the flora and fauna you find in woods and forests.

https://zenhabits.net/ Leo Babauta lives a life of minimalism, free from stress.

https://www.becomingminimalist.com/becoming-minimalist-start-here/ Joshua Becker's moment of revelation came when he was clearing out his garage. Another top minimalist guru.

https://www.mind.org.uk/information-support/types-of-mental-health-problems/depression/self-care-for-depression/#.WrUdi-jFLIU Several excellent ideas for self-care to boost your mood if you are feeling down.

https://www.forbes.com/sites/ilyapozin/2016/03/03/the-secret-to-happiness-spend-money-on-experiences-not-things/#1e8fbda739a6 Spend on experiences, never things.

http://feelhappiness.com/reframing-your-thoughts-make-yourself-happier/ Reframing made easy. The article has several examples of common situations when it might be useful to reframe your thoughts, like blaming yourself, dread of something bad happening and negative thoughts generally.

https://tinybuddha.com/blog/reframing-self-critical-thoughts-can-help-ease-anxiety/

An easy read for helping yourself deal with self-criticism that leads to anxiety.

www.quotescover.com: An easy to use computer site that gives you a wide variety of formats for making a quote ready to share as well as covers for Facebook, Twitter or other social sharing apps. Most of my quotes are created on this app.

www.pixabay.com: Free-to-use pictures to act as backgrounds for your quotes on the days you can't find what you need in your own space.

https://www.pinterest.co.uk/angeljem5/how-to-hygge-the-british-way-quotes/: Need a quote and you think I've used it? All the quotes from my books, blogs and more beside are on this board.

Inspirational Quotes One of many quote apps that are useful to have on your phone for daily inspiration..

Books

Scrumptious Treats For Vintage Housekeepers/ More Scrumptious Treats for Vintage Housekeepers by Alison May. Short ebooks that are lists of ideas, often free or cheap to do, to add a touch of self-care and ritual to your days. The lists are organised into topics such as 'Puttery Treats for Good Cheer' or 'Puttery Treats for Spring Cleaning'.

The Winter House/ The Spring House/ The Summer House/ The Autumn House by Alison May. Simple seasonal ideas to add beauty and joy to your routine. Each short book contains housekeeping ideas, self-care ideas, recipes and a short essay on the pleasures of the season.

Fika: The Art of the Swedish Coffee Break by Anna Brones and Johanna Kindvall. The why and how of Swedish Fika.

The Checklist Manifesto by Atul Gawande. If checklists can help a surgeon's work process move smoothly, it can probably benefit yours as well.

Live Lagom: Balanced Living the Swedish Way by Anna Brones

Lagom: The Swedish Art of Balanced Living by Linnea Dunne. Lagom is about creating balance across our lives. Both these books show us how that is achieved in Sweden and give us practical advice for how we can balance our lives to suit ourselves even if we're not Swedish.

Simple Abundance by Sarah Ban Breathnach. A self-care bible for most women. It's over 20 years old and still has wisdom for us to share.

Romancing The Ordinary by Sarah Ban Breathnach. Again, arranged seasonally, the book is designed to encourage us to make our lives more magical, to enchant ourselves into living authentically.

Dragonsinger: Harper of Pern by Anne McCaffrey. It's dragon fantasy, but this book, and the other two in the series, are about the young musician who fights against sexism to achieve her potential. I loved it as a teenager and still enjoy reading the series about the Dragonriders of Pern.

Flow: The Psychology of Happiness by Mihaly Csikszentmihalyi. The first book to talk about flow, and to recognise the power it plays in our lives.

How to Hygge Your Summer by Jo Kneale. Ideas to keep summer as happy and hyggely as possible.

The Lord Of The Rings by J R R Tolkien. Just because I love it.

Woodland Life (Usborne Spotter's Guide) A simple guide designed for children, but interesting enough for most beginners at recognizing and naming woodland creatures.

How to Be Human by Ruby Wax. A great guide to keeping your mind on the straight and narrow, written in Ruby Wax's inimitable style.

Reframe Your Viewpoints by Virginia Ritterbusch. How to make life better by changing the words you use about it.

Happiness At Christmastime:

It may be the Most Wonderful Time of the Year, according to a variety of singers, but Christmas can be a minefield for those of us looking to boost our happiness quotient. It's full of food, drink, families, bad weather, cramped quarters and so many decisions that we could have World War Three just deciding which channel to put on. If you're looking to be happier over Christmas, then you will have to be a little more selective about what you do at Christmastime. You can do it all, and have it all, just possibly not all at once in one year.

This chapter looks at ways of making this time of year simpler, and hopefully has good advice for making Christmas your way: happy, full of love and fun but without too much stress.

I have written about Christmas, and how to keep it hyggely, in another book, *Have Yourself a Happy, Hygge Christmas*, available from Amazon. It's full of ideas for celebrating Christmas at home and in work, and how to keep it as peaceful and enjoyable as you can for everyone concerned.

Live in the present, not for the present.

www.howtohyggethebritishway.com

Appreciate the seasons each in their turn

Live in each season as it passes; breathe the air, drink the drink, taste the fruit, and resign yourself to the influence of the earth. HenryDavidThoreau

www.howtohyggethebritishway.com

There is power in living in the season that you are in, and not racing towards the next season before the present one is half way through. Sadly, life isn't set up that way. It seems that life in the early 21st Century is all about how quickly we can get to the next big commercial festival. Back to school is cleared before August is over, Halloween fights for space with Christmas, which is speedily replaced by Easter eggs and Valentines chocolates before you can finish the panettone.

Magazines only exacerbate this movement, with the issue you receive at the end of one month often being dated for the month after next, if the release date falls badly. They have learned to put out issues early because consumers will buy the most up-to-date magazine on the shelf, even if that magazine is full of Easter bunnies as we walk through January snow.

I dislike this immensely. I frequently put aside those magazines that are trying to move me on to the next season too quickly and live with last month's issues read at the right time. I may have a quick flick through the diary pages to see if there is anything I need to book in advance, any workshops or exhibitions I would like to see, but otherwise I resist the urge to race. Time moves fast enough anyway, now I have finally admitted to middle-age.

I want to live my life in the season I am in. A few years ago, I found myself listening to a friend who was bemoaning the fact that it was January, and there was such a long time to go until the bright weather and summer sun. The year before, in summer time, she'd been bewailing the heat and the time left until Christmas. I thought, and still do, that we are so fortunate to get such clear seasons in the UK, we should be glad and live them fully. I think part of the reason I love hygge so much is that it makes enjoying the best of each season easier. In cold weather, drink chocolate and snuggle next to the fire, in spring go out and search for the crocus and daffodils. Summer is made for sitting and sipping cool drinks as the last rays of sun go down, or for crafting indoors as the rain pours on the roof. While Autumn is the King of seasons, a technicolour show of leaves and landscape that hint at life that has been and cold depths of winter to come.

Why is this chapter in the Christmas section of the book? Well, because Christmas is a season as much as winter, spring, summer or autumn are. We need to give each season their due, enjoy the gifts of each and make sure that we are not rushing towards any one of them at the peril of ignoring or failing to honour the one we are actually in. Live in the moment... even if that moment is cold.

Action:

❖ Make Could Do lists for the season ahead. These are lists that you might do, or might not get around to. I read of them first in The Simple Things magazine, and they are a lovely idea. See www.thesimplethings.com for more inspiration.

❖ Use Pinterest to gather ideas for activities that are season-specific. You can only catch leaves in autumn, find wild garlic in spring or plan to sit in the evening sun until 10pm in summer. Having activities to help you stay seasonal will help you to stay in the moment.

❖ The same with food: why not plan a seasonal month of meals? Use a website such as www.eatseasonably.co.uk to plan your meals around the best fruit and vegetables available. Imagine a salmon fillet served on a bed of roasted courgetti and red pepper followed by soft fruit salad and ice cream in July, or a pork casserole with apples and root vegetable mash in October. Eating seasonally prevents you getting into too deep a rut: it should also be better on your pocket and the environment.

❖ Read a seasonal almanac. In 2018, Lia Leendertz produced a beautiful book with moon phases, tide times, constellations of the month and other seasonal information to keep you grounded. I hope she produces one for every year. You can probably find a "Year of..." book for most areas of interest: birds, wildlife, gardening. Choose one that appeals and read it.

Anticipation is over half the fun.

There's something special about Christmas Eve, isn't there? I bet most of us can remember sitting there in excited anticipation, wondering what Father Christmas was going to bring us and hoping that the reindeers would be loud enough to wake us with their bells. I think nowadays Christmas Eve is even more fun for me than the Day itself. There's a point the night before where I sit, surrounded by baking and preparation, piles of presents neatly stacked under the tree, cup of tea in hand and I just feel so Christmassy.

I have learned to make it a ritual for the family, to make it a day of preparation and anticipation. We have work to do, ready for the next day, so there's a chores list with the banal and boring housekeeping listed there, but I aim to be finished by the time the sun sets and proper evening begins.

We light candles, watch family movies, unwrap new pyjamas and spend time together not busy, or racing, or aiming to achieve, just being. I read *The Story of Holly And Ivy* to my daughter after an easy, comfort food meal, and we all go to Midnight service at our church. It's the only time I ask my agnostic/atheist children to come with me. It's a valuable pause before the madness of Christmas Day.

Sad to say, when my children were young Christmas morning was an orgy of present ripping and an endless look for what next or what else. Look up 'Ungrateful Children at Christmas' on YouTube and be prepared to watch over-tired and hangry young people cry their way past the best their parents could offer. I'm betting in years to come they'll look back at Christmas Eve with nostalgic memories and wipe the morning itself from their minds.

Christmas Eve was a night of song that wrapped itself about you like a shawl. But it warmed more than your body. It warmed your heart...filled it, too, with melody that would last forever.

Bess Streeter Aldrich

www.howtohyggethebritishway.com

The anticipation of an event or expected purchase can often be better than the event itself. It doesn't really exist anywhere apart from our hearts, we have to use all our powers of imagination to summon up the sights, sounds, feels that we expect and hope to feel. It's like positive thinking+++. To a certain extent the actual event is bound to fall short, since reality and imagination very rarely match. That's why building anticipation into our lives, and especially at this time of year, is important. The longer we can experience that joy and the pleasure of imagined delights, the more joy and pleasure we get out of a thing regardless of whether or not it's a success.

The Year of Drear (my last year in school) I found that, more than ever, I needed the anticipation of Christmas, or holidays or special occasions to give me something to look forward to. They were the gems I held onto when nobody talked to me, the golden thoughts that I summoned up in long, cold playtimes spent in solitude. I know at the time I worried I was wishing my life away (six weeks to Christmas... five weeks to half term... four weeks until Easter) but looking back I think that anticipation and positive belief that I had good times ahead was part of what kept me going.

I'm perfectly happy now, but anticipation is still a big part of my life. I like having something to look forward to, to dream about, to plan for. A weekend break, a family party or an evening scheduled to spend with a friend all feed my happy space.

Action

- ❖ Try and have all your Christmas preparation done before hand so that you can sit and enjoy Christmas Eve. Have a traditional meal that you eat (we find roast ham works well, and gives us a choice of meats for the lunchtime sandwich on Boxing Day), a film that you always watch or a book that you read. Sometimes it's only when Kermit the Frog sings "There's Only One More Sleep 'Til Christmas" that the excitement of the next day is free to begin.
- ❖ Make a ritual of Christmas Eve. Have a Christmas Eve box: pack new pyjamas into it, a choice of nibbles, a new book for everybody (as they do in Iceland), reindeer food to sprinkle on the path and perhaps a game or DVD to watch as a family. After your evening meal, open the box, and let the magic wash over you.
- ❖ Carry anticipation through the year as well. Always have something you can look forward to, such as a party, a meal out or a day trip or theatre trip. If your budget is exceedingly tight, look out for free events or sales on train tickets that will let you plan a trip. We never stay anywhere but Travelodge, where rooms for pretty much anywhere except central London can often be picked up quite cheaply.

Christmas planning

Christmas comes at the same time each year. Indeed, it's so regular that it happens on the same date every year. And knowing that means that planning for it should be easier than planning for an event that gets dropped in your lap at the last moment.

I find Christmas an absolute pleasure, and always have done, but when I first got married the thought of being responsible for Christmas for a household was intimidating. How much food did I need? Whose pattern of Christmas was best? What events and traditions did we want to do as a family, and indeed who counted as family for the meal?

I spent a couple of years running around like a headless chicken at Christmas, trying to fit everything in, please everyone and give everybody the Christmas I thought they wanted. It worked, too, for a couple of years, but then the inevitable happened and I was ill over Christmas. It was a smaller, simpler, easier affair that year and the contrast was amazing. I didn't need to do the obligation calls, nobody rang to ask where their handmade Christmas cards were, and the Christmas meal I eventually prepared was small, but simply enough.

> # Christmas is a tonic for our souls. It moves us to think of others rather than of ourselves. It directs our thoughts to giving.
>
> B. C. Forbes

www.howtohyggethebritishway.com

My planning for Christmas improved dramatically after that. I jettisoned a lot of obligations and decided that I would make my Christmas run to suit only me and my family. I set out to plan ahead as much as possible, so that when December came I would be free to enjoy the shops without the pain of purchasing, free to enjoy movies on TV without thinking I had to clean or declutter for company and free to do only those Christmas activities that gave me joy.

It took a few years, but I now have my Christmas planning running like a well-oiled machine. I have a planning notebook that comes out every September (yes, my Christmas starts that early) and into which I note the presents I have to buy, the events we are committed to and the meals, shopping and sundry other lists that make up a modern Christmas. I have lists for shopping arranged by date, arranged by shop and arranged by person. I have menu plans that go back years and just need tweaking. I even, in my Evernote Christmas notebook, have lists of presents going back over the last 5 years to try and avoid repetition as much as possible.

If planning has never been a big part of your Christmases, then take a look at www.organizedhome.com for ideas on creating a Christmas planner that will guide you through. Start early, and use the planner well.

Action:

❖ Find a notebook or folder to use as your Christmas planner.

❖ Look online for ideas to set up your Christmas planner. You may not need every page that different websites have, but one activity that you do need to do is set out what your ideal Christmas looks like and feels like so that you can identify the elements you need to plan for.

❖ Two books that I have found helpful with organising the season are *A Chic and Simple Christmas* by Fiona Ferris and *The Christmas Countdown* by Alison May. They helped me think though an ideal Christmas and let me set out to have a celebration that suited my family, rather than any external image of Christmas.

Christmas is a time to enjoy others: so take the time!

When we think of Christmas, we usually think of it as a time of togetherness. Idealised pictures of Christmas usually show families gathered together around the tree or a fantastically prepared Christmas dinner. We travel the country to reach relatives and spend time with them, we do our best to ask relatives who may be alone to spend time with us.

Christmas is a time to spend with others, for many of us. It's a time to embrace the full house, the noise and the spectacle of three (or more) generations playing cards and arguing over the remote.

Christmas is, above all, a day of interruptions. Well-meaning, but interruptions nevertheless

Nigel Slater

www.howtohyggethebritishway.co.uk

That doesn't mean it needs to be stress, stress, stress all the way, though. It's very easy to end up with a house full of people and see no way through to December 27th, when they're all due to leave. Be sensible: if Christmas is the season of goodwill and peace to all mankind, that includes you as well. Don't be a Christmas Martyr. Plan the season as early as possible, don't be afraid to delegate, make lists of chores and share them out. And let people look after themselves as much as you can.

To properly enjoy visitors you need to give them (and you) some space to breathe. If there's not enough room downstairs for a quiet seating area, them perhaps there's just space in a bedroom for a chair and a spare TV. Set up the guest bedroom with a small kettle, teabags, coffee and mugs, just like a hotel room, and your guests can sidle off for a quiet rest sometime.

If your guests are children or young adults, set up a play area or games zone in a spare space. Even the garage would work, as long as it's draught free and could hold a few chairs, perhaps a table, and the entertainment needed. We have a darts board and a small size snooker table in our garage. Mis-spent youth? No, we got those in my middle age!

Don't be afraid to get other people helping either. Those pesky vegetables or potatoes aren't going to peel themselves, are they? Either plan meals for every night yourself and allocate roles in the cooking/cleaning teams, or agree to take turns at preparation and leave your guests in charge of preparing a meal for you. Take the breaks you are offered and run with them. There are no prizes ever for being a martyr!

Different families do different things at Christmas. We love board games and movies, so our entertainment features them heavily. Other families see Christmas Day especially as day to switch off the TV and do other stuff. Whatever your style, relax and enjoy the occasion.

Action:

- ❖ Advance planning is key to a relaxed Christmas. I like to have everything I need ready for the day before Christmas Eve, so that I can have a full three-day holiday without major stress during Christmas. The madness before means I can relax more during.

- ❖ Don't forget the little touches that welcome guests into the house: new soap, fresh towels, a space to help themselves to drinks or treats.

❖ Never apologise for your house, children or anything. True friends won't care, and the people that care aren't worth the self-flagellation of apologizing anyway. The house, the family, you… you are what you are, and you don't need to put on a show for Christmas unless you really want to.

Post-Christmas is a time made for hygge

In Norway, the period between Christmas and New Year's Eve is called Romjul. Rather cutely, there's a push to call it Twixtmas in the UK. It's a week when a lot of people aren't at work, the children are off school, the decorations are still up, you can't do much except sit and rest. It's a hygge hibernation week.

In seed time learn, in harvest teach, in winter enjoy.

William Blake

www.howtohyggethebritishway.co.uk

I love this week in the year, it's one of my favourites. You may have people to go and visit, or have visitors yourself, but work and responsibility can go hang for a short while.

And although I am a complete fan of hibernation (you only have to read my blog between January and February to see that) I also want to come into the next new year ready for action.

When I was a little girl, I always used to get a diary at Christmas, usually a Brownie diary, small and with a little pencil that slid in the spine. With a steady diet of old movies on the Tv, a pile of presents to enjoy and a diary to fill in, the space between gave me the chance to get ahead for the next year.

I still like to treat myself to a diary or calendar for Christmas now, and Romjul is still my chance to plan ahead. I like to take some time, to set aside a day or two to slow down and think over the past and then plan the future. I make a ritual of it, sitting in my hygge corner, basket of pens and books to hand and fill in what I know to be true: future events, dates or times of the year when I know I need to look at decorating the house or doing the garden.

I set my intention for the year, aiming to be more of something: happier, more relaxed, more resilient. Something that I have identified as missing from my life generally. I might take the time to write out the word and decorate it, or search out an image that captures the essence of what I'm looking for.

But I don't spend all my time between Christmas and New Year navel gazing. It's one of the few times when the whole family are free to be together, with no school or work to come between us. I plan trips, perhaps, like a theatre trip or cinema trip, but mostly we hygge together. Even better if the weather is cold and snowy, we wake late and get up for brunch most days. Cooking is kept simple on purpose, with a lot of Christmas left-overs. Soup for lunch is a favourite, and turkey and ham pie for tea.

We always get a DVD each as part of our Christmas presents so as a family we have five movies to see us through Romjul. With popcorn and chocolates, it makes for an easy week of evening entertainment. Depending on the weather, it can be easier than a cinema trip anyway.

Last Christmas we booked a break away as a family. It was three days and two nights lost from our Romjul. Never again. We were cross, tired and we missed the slobbery of not getting dressed until we felt like it, not going out unless we wanted to and, surprisingly for me, the last of the leftovers meals. Romjul should be a time to barricade yourself against the world, to hygge with the family, eat the wrong stuff, do the jigsaws, go on windy walks and basically just be.

Action:
- ❖ Plan for Romjul in your Christmas planning. Choose easy meals, or plan to have leftovers and stock up beforehand. Hide a box or two of chocolates, as well, so that there are some treats to eat after Christmas Day.
- ❖ Give yourself permission just to be. If you have a family, stop and watch them playing rather than drag them out to do stuff. Better yet, get down on the floor and play with them. It's good to let your inner child go free now and again.
- ❖ If you are an organised person, then make time this week to set up your diary and calendar. Start looking at things you might want to do in the months ahead and pencil them in. There's no better feeling than starting the new year with a clean diary.

Let things go. A New Year Cleansing ritual prepares you for the next challenge.

How was your year? Good? Bad? A bit of both? Did you have some goals penciled in that you achieved or did not achieve? Some things that happened to destroy your equilibrium? Life is never perfect: Life is not fair, and anyone that tells you otherwise is trying to sell you something (The Princess Bride, one of my favourite films) so there will always be something that happens that upsets/angers/debilitates you.

Somewhere on the internet there will be a service or a group that can provide real help for most problems, and if you are in danger/debt or suffering at the hand of anyone else, then I'd ask you to find that help as soon as you can. If, on the other hand, your problems are more manageable and were irritations rather than massive issues, a year-end cleansing ritual could be a useful way to clear them from your psyche and off your mind.

I have done this a few times in the past at times of particular stress and it does give your brain a very physical sign that the year is over, and all the problems of last year have been put behind you.

Very simply, take an hour to clean out your brain.

List all the issues that have held you back on a slip of paper. Put down any negative thoughts, any negative talk, issues that have kept you awake, failed projects that you have now abandoned, negative feelings or emotions that you have. You can even list the people who are holding you back or making you feel negative. You can write just a plain list, or record the feelings and emotions connected to the items. What you are aiming for is to get all the negative in your life onto a piece of paper.

Now, go outside into your garden and take the paper and a metal baking dish with you, something heat-proof. You are going to crumple up the paper first, then rip into pieces, then put in the dish and finally set light to it. All the time, imagine that the dark feelings are leaving your body. Imagine a light entering your soul, burning off the negative and leaving only the positive. Release your negative, free yourself from the judgements that we very easily make about ourselves. Say out loud "I forgive myself".

As the bad from last year burns away, state your positive intentions. Make sure they are positive, for example "I will be healthy by exercising three times a week" rather than "I will not put weight on." You may want to list your positive attributes, to identify the facets of your character that are positive and that you want to nourish. Go in, and write a list of these. Keep them somewhere safe, where you can see them regularly and reward yourself with a hug when you read them.

Finally, hug yourself. Tell your inner being that you will face yourself with truth, compassion and appreciation. Drink a toast to your new self, then go in and clean the house. Clean inside, clean outside.

Cleansing rituals at times of rebirth have often been a part of many religions. The Jewish faith has a total top-to-bottom house cleaning ready for Passover, even to the tiniest corner of the kitchen cupboards, using a feather. In India, people traditionally immerse themselves in the waters of the Ganges at new year, while in Myanmar all the statues of Buddha are scrubbed clean during the festival of Thingyan when every inhabitant, every building and dwelling place is drenched in cleansing water.

Action:

- ❖ Perform the cleansing ritual. See how it makes you feel. If you like it, and feel better, then do it again next year. You have very little to lose, and a lot to gain.

- ❖ Want a deeper cleanse? Then do a house cleaning session. Pick an area that needs cleaning, like a room or a cupboard, and set to work. Focus on your issues as you scrub, and watch them melt away. The exercise involved in cleaning and the mental release of scrubbing away your problems will give you a brighter spirit to face the next day with.

- ❖ Read A Monk's Guide to A Clean House And Mind to see how getting your externals to the point of perfect cleanliness feeds into your internal self as well.

Start The New Year With Good Intentions

Winter is a time to pause, reflect and renew for the coming Spring. Our Creator partnered with Nature and with infinite wisdom, designed this time for you to reflect on your life, set new goals and look at what needs to change.

Eileen Anglin

www.howtohyggethebritishway.co.uk

The New Year is often seen as a great time to set out your goals and intentions again. There is something about the year changing that gives us an impetus to make a change, perhaps because we become aware of the movement of time. I never believed my Nan when she said that time moves faster when you get older, but it does. Now is a good time to check that your goals and your life values are working together, that they will move your life forward and they're not going to be so unachievable that you will drop them by the third week in January. Look at the chapter, Set A Goal And Write It Down, for advice on goals that are realistic and achievable.

I hate making New Year Resolutions, so I make sure my goals at this time are totally achievable and not so worthy that I will lose interest in them. I keep my aims small, and make sure I include the silly things of life that make living worthwhile... like a monthly catch up with a good friend, or marking some free time off in the work calendar as something else, like 'appointment at MH', so that it looks totally official and cannot be cancelled. (MH stands for Mental Health)

I also like making a wishlist of things I want to do during the year/s ahead. These can be epic journeys, small trips, reading or watching something, getting out twice a week or anything that I want to see, do, learn, watch, make or visit. I keep this in my notebook or planner and update it regularly. The items aren't time-specific, often, so if I get them done or don't get them done it won't matter.   My wishlist this year includes travelling to Copenhagen, finally seeing Wicked the musical, spending more time with my parents, a week by the sea and reading as many of Dickens' novels as I can. It's the 150th anniversary of his death on 9th June 2020 so I have set that as a possible end date to complete that challenge by! I won't be desolate if I don't achieve all of these by the end of the year, I'll just transfer them over to next year's list, if I still want to do them.

And then... I just do them. Not all at once, and not all of them. But I know if someone offers to come to see a play or a movie on my list, I tick it off and go happily. If the chance for a daytrip or short break comes up, I say yes. Knowing what I want to do gives me the freedom to say yes or no, depending on whether what's offered suits me. It makes my decision-making process simpler.

Action:

- ❖ Writing down resolutions or goals makes you much more likely to achieve them, research shows, so write down your goals for the next year. Keep them in your planner or post on a cupboard door. Look at them often, and update them when you need to. The list you needed in December may not be the list you need in July.
- ❖ Make a wishlist of things to do. It's like a bucket list, but without the bad diagnosis. Change it and edit it to suit what you like doing. No lists should ever be set in stone.

Get Ready For Hibernation

Part of every January and February is my hibernation time: when the weather is bad enough to keep you at home, the Christmas decorations are down and the cold winter drags on, making you feel it will never stop.

For a few years I participated in Beauty That Moves' Online Hibernate retreat, but last winter I drew up my own hibernation plan. You can read about it on my blog, How to Hygge The British Way, by looking up #hibernate2018.

Hibernation is about taking time out to care for yourself. January and February are often quiet times in the year, not many events, not many people are away on holiday and they have a stillness after the month of madness that is Christmas. It's a good time to read a couple of self-help books, start a craft project or finish one that has been on the back burner and to establish habits that will help you feel happier over the year.

Last winter I focused on five areas of my life: crafting, reading, cooking, self-care and company, or building better relationships.

I wanted to boost my creativity so I set out to read *Art and Soul Reloaded* by Pam Grout. This is a year-long apprenticeship, it said, so I read only a little. I planned ahead and stocked up on craft goodies and books to read during the last long nights of Winter. A quiet evening spent crocheting or sewing is an evening well spent.

I found making my diet healthier was an interesting challenge. I like to plan wholesome stews and soups that cook all day in the slow cooker, or in the oven, building more vegetables into my meal planning, through side dishes or soups and stews. There were several recipes I tried for the first time that have become family favourites.

Hibernation is a survival strategy designed to conserve energy when conditions are harsh.

How Stuff Works

www.howtohyggethebritishway.co.uk

Of course, hibernating is a very hyggely thing to do. I have a cosy home anyway, but I made sure there was a hyggely level of light, usually by using fairy lights and table lamps instead of an overhead light, and that the rooms were warm without being suffocatingly so. I also tried to make sure I got outside as much as possible, with daytime walks and open windows to air the house. It's no use relaxing at home if you never stir from it long enough to appreciate the warmth when you get back.

By the end of February I was relaxed and peaceful. I could see the benefit of slowing down. My summers can be as hectic as they like: hibernating during the coldest, darkest part of the year has built up my happiness store.

Action:

❖ Draw up your own list ready for the middle of winter. Start thinking of the crafts to do and books you'd love to read when the cold wind blows and you need a break.

❖ Look out for online retreats and courses in mindfulness, hygge or wellbeing. Self-paced ones let you do them when you have the time, but a guided course can also be useful.

❖ Use your evenings well. Not a crafter? Try writing, learning a language or a musical instrument, watching a series that you wouldn't normally try or doing an exercise class from Youtube.

Happiness At Christmas Time Resources

Websites and Articles

www.thesimplethings.com: A beautiful magazine, with a lovely blog and plenty of ideas for living well all year round.

www.eatseasonably.co.uk: To ensure that the food you are eating is the best quality you can have, this website sets out what is in season for every month.

http://organizedhome.com/ has plenty of printables, including everything you need to set up a working Christmas planner.

https://www.the-pool.com/life/life-honestly/2016/52/lauren-bravo-on-her-mum-being-the-queen-of-romjul Brilliant and evocative piece on Romjul... what it is and how to do it properly.

http://www.twixtmas.com/ Want your Twixtmas to be good for you and others? This website has ideas for using that time profitably.

http://www.calmmoment.com/mindfulness/how-to-make-positive-new-years-resolutions-and-set-goals-for-2018/ Good advice for setting resolutions that will work

http://jackcanfield.com/blog/my-101-lifetime-goals-list-and-why-you-should-have-one-too/: Jack Canfield is an expert at goal setting and making money from it. This article explains how to have a life list and dream big.

https://zenhabits.net/a-simple-guide-to-setting-and-achieving-your-life-goals/: Leo Babauta shows how to take that life list and make it work by looking back from where you want to be.

http://www.calmmoment.com/mindfulness/how-to-make-positive-new-years-resolutions-and-set-goals-for-2018/ Advice on writing a wishlist for the year, rather than a list of resolutions.

http://beautythatmoves.typepad.com/beauty_that_moves/2017/12/hibernate-online-retreat.html Usually runs an online retreat in the first few weeks of the year, with a variety of crafts, cookery and homemaking ideas.

https://howtohyggethebritishway.com/tag/hibernate2018/ My blog, with last year's hibernate retreat that I designed for myself. Creating it to suit your own preferences is a way to guarantee that it will all suit you.

Books and Films

Have Yourself a Happy, Hygge Christmas by Jo Kneale. Hey, if I can't shamelessly promote my own books now and again, what is the point of being a writer? Besides, this is a beautifully easy read on why you should be selfish at Christmas and how to keep your season happier.

The Almanac: A Seasonal Guide to 2018 by Lia Leendertz

The Muppet Christmas Carol (DVD) is one of the best versions of A Christmas Carol out there. Believe me, if you don't know this movie, it is brilliant.

A Chic And Simple Christmas by Fiona Ferris. Simple ways to enjoy the season your way. Fiona's version of how she stopped doing what was expected and did what she needed to instead is worth a read.

The Christmas Countdown by Alison May. Thirty days to plan, organise and enjoy a Christmas full of puttery treats and loveliness. Don't know what a puttery treat is? Fie! Go over to Google and search for puttery treats. Then indulge in a few, guilt free.

The Princess Bride (DVD) makes this list simply because it has so many good quotes that you can use through the whole of your life. It's an absolute classic.

Art And Soul Reloaded by Pam Grout.

A Monk's Guide to A Clean House And Mind by Shoukei Matsumoto. Having a clean, minimal home helps your inner being be clean and minimal as well.

Many Thanks

Writing a book, even if you're writing and publishing it solo like I am, takes a lot of support. This book has taken longer and was harder to write than my first few, I think because it is so much more wide-reaching and takes in a lot more aspects of life. It's also a lot more personal than my books on hygge, because happiness and seeking to be happier is a lot more personal.

I couldn't have written it without a great deal of help from various sources:

To my Hygge Nook friends on Facebook. You're always ready with advice or a wise answer when I need you. Your daily posts of happiness and hygge keep me balanced when I am getting too busy to think.

To my friends, especially Claire Smith. Wise woman, and always ready to share Prosecco and talk about why happiness is better than sadness.

To my extended family. Mum, Dad, Andy, Chris, Jon, Pat, Jane, Joanne and all the nieces and nephews who always look impressed when I say I'm writing a book. You're all a big reason for my happiness.

To my wonderful children, David, James and Sarah. You make me truly happy, and you put up with me being a bad mother again and again. It's a good job you've grown up so sensible, or really there'd be nothing out for you.

And finally to Peter, my best friend, best employer and best husband. You've supported me writing this book with your patience, advice and letting me have the use of your front office cost-free. You always make me really happy. I love you so much.

No... not finally... that final thanks should be to you, the reader, for buying or stealing this book, reading it and, hopefully, enjoying it. I know I'd be writing anyway, but it's even nicer knowing that there are people out there reading my words. Thank you so much, and Bless you all x

Jo Kneale

will return again

in Autumn 2018

with a book, probably about Christmas planning.

Don't get too excited, then.

Printed in Great Britain
by Amazon